Suicide
Opposing Viewpoints®

OTHER BOOKS OF RELATED INTEREST

OPPOSING VIEWPOINTS SERIES

Abortion

AIDS

An Aging Population

Biomedical Ethics

Civil Liberties

Constructing a Life Philosophy

The Death Penalty

Death & Dying

Euthanasia

Gun Control

Homosexuality

Mental Illness

Paranormal Phenomena

CURRENT CONTROVERSIES SERIES

The Disabled

Ethics

Gun Control

Hunger

Reproductive Technologies

AT ISSUE SERIES

The Spread of AIDS

Suicide

Opposing Viewpoints®

David L. Bender, *Publisher*

Bruno Leone, *Executive Editor*

Brenda Stalcup, *Managing Editor*

Scott Barbour, *Senior Editor*

Tamara L. Roleff, *Book Editor*

OPPOSING
VIEWPOINTS®
SERIES

Greenhaven Press, Inc., San Diego, California

Cover photo: Craig MacLain

Library of Congress Cataloging-in-Publication Data

Suicide : opposing viewpoints / Tamara L. Roleff, book editor.
    p.   cm. — (Opposing viewpoints series)
  Includes bibliographical references and index.
  ISBN 1-56510-665-2 (lib.). — ISBN 1-56510-664-4 (pbk.)
  1. Suicide—United States. 2. Suicide—Moral and ethical aspects. 3.
Teenagers—Suicidal behavior—United States. I. Roleff, Tamara L.,
1959–   . II. Series: Opposing viewpoints series (Unnumbered)
HV6548.U5S88 1998
362.28—dc21   97-6697
                                                                  CIP

Greenhaven Press, Inc., P.O. Box 289009
San Diego, CA 92198-9009

"CONGRESS SHALL MAKE NO LAW... ABRIDGING THE FREEDOM OF SPEECH, OR OF THE PRESS."

First Amendment to the U.S. Constitution

The basic foundation of our democracy is the First Amendment guarantee of freedom of expression. The Opposing Viewpoints Series is dedicated to the concept of this basic freedom and the idea that it is more important to practice it than to enshrine it.

CONTENTS

WHY CONSIDER OPPOSING VIEWPOINTS?

"The only way in which a human being can make some approach to knowing the whole of a subject is by hearing what can be said about it by persons of every variety of opinion and studying all modes in which it can be looked at by every character of mind. No wise man ever acquired his wisdom in any mode but this."

John Stuart Mill

In our media-intensive culture it is not difficult to find differing opinions. Thousands of newspapers and magazines and dozens of radio and television talk shows resound with differing points of view. The difficulty lies in deciding which opinion to agree with and which "experts" seem the most credible. The more inundated we become with differing opinions and claims, the more essential it is to hone critical reading and thinking skills to evaluate these ideas. Opposing Viewpoints books address this problem directly by presenting stimulating debates that can be used to enhance and teach these skills. The varied opinions contained in each book examine many different aspects of a single issue. While examining these conveniently edited opposing views, readers can develop critical thinking skills such as the ability to compare and contrast authors' credibility, facts, argumentation styles, use of persuasive techniques, and other stylistic tools. In short, the Opposing Viewpoints Series is an ideal way to attain the higher-level thinking and reading skills so essential in a culture of diverse and contradictory opinions.

In addition to providing a tool for critical thinking, Opposing Viewpoints books challenge readers to question their own strongly held opinions and assumptions. Most people form their opinions on the basis of upbringing, peer pressure, and personal, cultural, or professional bias. By reading carefully balanced opposing views, readers must directly confront new ideas as well as the opinions of those with whom they disagree. This is not to simplistically argue that everyone who reads opposing views will—or should—change his or her opinion. Instead, the series enhances readers' understanding of their own views by encouraging confrontation with opposing ideas. Careful examination of others' views can lead to the readers' understanding of the logical inconsistencies in their own opinions, perspective on why they hold an opinion, and the consideration of the possibility that their opinion requires further evaluation.

EVALUATING OTHER OPINIONS

To ensure that this type of examination occurs, Opposing Viewpoints books present all types of opinions. Prominent spokespeople on different sides of each issue as well as well-known professionals from many disciplines challenge the reader. An additional goal of the series is to provide a forum for other, less known, or even unpopular viewpoints. The opinion of an ordinary person who has had to make the decision to cut off life support from a terminally ill relative, for example, may be just as valuable and provide just as much insight as a medical ethicist's professional opinion. The editors have two additional purposes in including these less known views. One, the editors encourage readers to respect others' opinions—even when not enhanced by professional credibility. It is only by reading or listening to and objectively evaluating others' ideas that one can determine whether they are worthy of consideration. Two, the inclusion of such viewpoints encourages the important critical thinking skill of objectively evaluating an author's credentials and bias. This evaluation will illuminate an author's reasons for taking a particular stance on an issue and will aid in readers' evaluation of the author's ideas.

As series editors of the Opposing Viewpoints Series, it is our hope that these books will give readers a deeper understanding of the issues debated and an appreciation of the complexity of even seemingly simple issues when good and honest people disagree. This awareness is particularly important in a democratic society such as ours in which people enter into public debate to determine the common good. Those with whom one disagrees should not be regarded as enemies but rather as people whose views deserve careful examination and may shed light on one's own.

Thomas Jefferson once said that "difference of opinion leads to inquiry, and inquiry to truth." Jefferson, a broadly educated man, argued that "if a nation expects to be ignorant and free . . . it expects what never was and never will be." As individuals and as a nation, it is imperative that we consider the opinions of others and examine them with skill and discernment. The Opposing Viewpoints Series is intended to help readers achieve this goal.

David L. Bender & Bruno Leone,
Series Editors

INTRODUCTION

"Sometimes the most difficult thing in the world is to choose to endure life."
Edwin S. Shneidman, The Suicidal Mind, 1996

In May 1996, the U.S. Navy's top admiral, Jeremy "Mike" Boorda, committed suicide when he learned that *Newsweek* magazine wanted to question him about the legitimacy of two of his medals. Earlier in his career, Boorda had worn "V" pins (for valor) on two medals, indicating that he had served under fire during the Vietnam War. Although Boorda served in the Vietnam theater, his medal citations did not authorize him to wear the "V" pins. Boorda stopped wearing the pins about a year before his death when a friend pointed out that he was not entitled to wear them. According to Boorda's suicide note, wearing the pins was an honest mistake.

Much of the nation was shocked over Boorda's suicide; many felt it was an irrational overreaction to a minor mistake that had been corrected. Yet others—especially those who have served in the military—believed his suicide was the honorable way out of a potential scandal. Peter J. Boyer of the *New Yorker* editorialized that Boorda died "a warrior's death" because he feared the *Newsweek* exposé would bring dishonor on the navy in which he had served for forty years.

Choosing death before dishonor is seen by some philosophers and ethicists as a rational reason to commit suicide. According to these experts, committing suicide can be a rational, morally permissible, and sometimes even obligatory act. Victor Cosculluela, author of *The Ethics of Suicide*, contends that suicide is rational and permissible if it serves as an expression of one's deepest values or as an escape from an unbearable existence. Suicide is obligatory, he continues, if it will protect others from death or suffering, such as a soldier falling on a grenade or a pilot crashing a disabled plane into a hill to avoid a field full of children.

Many health care professionals agree that suicide can be a rational decision if certain conditions are met. A 1995 study by James L. Werth and Debra C. Cobia found that 88 percent of two hundred psychologists they surveyed supported the concept of rational suicide if the person considering suicide has a terminal illness, is in severe physical or psychological pain, or is experiencing an unacceptable quality of life and freely chooses to die.

The researchers also stipulate that in order for a decision to commit suicide to be considered rational, the individual must have met with a mental health professional, weighed all the alternatives, considered how the act would affect others, and consulted with friends, family members, and clergy.

But other health care professionals believe that suicide can never be a rational choice. Leon R. Kass, an ethicist, physician, and outspoken critic of the right-to-die movement, argues that the determination to kill oneself is often made in response to feelings of guilt, fear, despair, or rejection. Suicide in these situations may be understandable and even forgivable, he asserts, but it is still an irrational and emotional response. Furthermore, because death is unimaginable, Kass contends, one cannot accurately judge whether death would be preferable to life. Therefore, he concludes, to choose death cannot possibly be a rational decision:

> Do we know what we are talking about when we claim that someone can *rationally* choose nonbeing or nothingness? How can poor reason even contemplate nothingness, much less accurately calculate its merits as compared with continued existence?

Author Joyce Carol Oates agrees: "Rationally one cannot 'choose' Death because Death is an unknown experience, and perhaps it isn't even an 'experience'—perhaps it is simply nothing; and one cannot imagine nothing." Oates and Kass assert that the merits of other actions can be imagined because it is possible to discuss them with people who have experienced them; death, however, is totally unknowable.

Others contend that choosing death as an escape from life's troubles is cowardly and selfish. For example, some maintain that Boorda's suicide was a cowardly act because he did not consider how his action would affect his wife, his children, and his reputation. Pat Smith, who wrote a letter to *Newsweek*, asks,

> What is honorable, manly or brave about shooting yourself rather than taking the heat for your own deliberate actions? What regard did he show for his wife and children, wounding their hearts with his death?

Others concur, arguing that Boorda's suicide and the circumstances surrounding it were more dishonorable than the act of wearing medals he did not deserve.

Whether Boorda's decision to commit suicide was rational and honorable or cowardly and irrational, his death was just one of an estimated thirty-one thousand suicides in 1996. As the number of suicides continues to increase each year, society struggles to understand and respond to this troubling trend. The authors in *Suicide: Opposing Viewpoints* examine ethical and legal issues as well as arguments concerning the cause and prevention of suicide in the following chapters: Is Suicide an Individual Right? What Are the Causes of Teen Suicide? Should Assisted Suicide Be Legal? How Can Suicide Be Prevented? The contributors to these chapters shed light on the emotional and sensitive issues involved in the national discussion on suicide.

CHAPTER 1

IS SUICIDE AN
INDIVIDUAL RIGHT?

CHAPTER PREFACE

Forty-nine states have passed laws regulating assisted suicide; forty-eight of them prohibit the practice. Only Oregon permits physicians to help their terminally ill patients commit suicide. In January 1997, the U.S. Supreme Court heard two cases, *Compassion in Dying v. State of Washington* (also known as *Glucksberg v. Washington*) and *Quill v. Vacco*, which had overturned state laws in Washington and New York banning assisted suicide. At the time of this writing, the Supreme Court's decision was expected in the summer of 1997.

The *Compassion in Dying* case began in 1994, when three terminally ill patients (who have since died); their doctor, Harold Glucksberg; and the right-to-die organization Compassion in Dying filed suit against the state of Washington. The plaintiffs argued that the state's ban on physician-assisted suicide violated the patients' right of due process and placed an undue burden on terminally ill people who wanted to hasten their deaths with a doctor's help. A Seattle district judge ruled in the patients' favor. When the state appealed to the Ninth U.S. Circuit Court of Appeals, a three-judge panel overturned the decision. In a rare move, the circuit court voted to hear the case again *en banc*, or in front of the entire court. In March 1996, the court ruled 8 to 3 in favor of Glucksberg and Compassion in Dying. The case went to the U.S. Supreme Court when the state of Washington appealed.

A month later, the Second U.S. Circuit Court of Appeals found New York's law against physician-assisted suicide unconstitutional. Timothy E. Quill, a physician who had assisted in the suicide of a patient, had challenged the law, claiming it violated the equal protection clause of the U.S. Constitution. The court agreed and overturned the ban. Dennis C. Vacco, as the state attorney general, appealed the ruling to the U.S. Supreme Court.

The Supreme Court's ruling in these two cases will determine the legality of assisted suicide laws in forty-nine states. The authors in the following chapter debate the issue being considered by the nation's highest court: whether individuals have a right to commit suicide and whether that right is protected by the U.S. Constitution.

> "It is not clear on what grounds a government, or anyone else, could be entitled to prevent a competent person from controlling the duration of his or her life."

SUICIDE IS AN INDIVIDUAL RIGHT

Ernest van den Haag

Ernest van den Haag argues in the following viewpoint that individuals—as the owners of their own bodies—have the right to determine whether or not to end their lives through suicide. Moreover, van den Haag maintains, no one has the right to compel someone to live against his or her will. Van den Haag is a psychoanalyst, the John M. Olin Professor Emeritus of Jurisprudence and Public Policy at Fordham University in Bronx, New York, and a scholar at the Heritage Foundation, a conservative public policy think tank in Washington, D.C.

As you read, consider the following questions:

1. In van den Haag's opinion, why should physicians be excluded from an individual's decision to commit suicide?
2. What is odd about society's attitude toward the disabled who want to commit suicide, according to the author?
3. Why is the "slippery slope" argument against assisted suicide irrational, in van den Haag's opinion?

B efore Christianity, governments were unconcerned with suicide, which was thought expedient in some circumstances and required by honor in others. However, with the coming of Christianity suicide became a sin, a violation of God's commandments. As unrepentant sinners, suicides were denied burial in consecrated ground and expected to end in Hell. Life was thought to be a gift from God, Who ordained its beginning and end. We possessed the life created by Him, but He owned it. Our possession could not license us to destroy what did not belong to us.

As the grip of Christianity weakened, this part of religion was secularized, as were many others. Suicide became a transgression against nature, not God, usually explained by mental derangement. Absent derangement, suicide was considered a crime against society, thought to own individuals more or less as God had been thought to before. Only in our time has it come to be believed that individuals collectively own society, rather than vice versa. They also are thought to own themselves. Without God (or slavery) no one else really could. Owners can dispose of what they own as they see fit. We thus each become entitled to control our life, including its duration, to the extent nature permits, provided that this control does not harm others in ways proscribed by law.

MANY OBSTACLES

Very few people are inclined to commit suicide. But this hardly seems a good reason to prevent it, although sometimes it is asserted or implied that the unpopularity of suicide argues for its immorality and for preventing it. Yet, those who do not wish, or do not feel they have the moral right, to end their life can easily refrain. It is not clear on what grounds a government, or anyone else, could be entitled to prevent a competent person from controlling the duration of his or her life.

Although the foregoing view seems irrefutable, not everyone accepts it. It is contrary to tradition, wherefore many obstacles remain in the way of people who try to shorten their life. These obstacles can be nearly insurmountable for those who most wish to do so because of a disabling disease. They may be forced to go on living against their will. Even some healthy persons find the obstacles quite forbidding. They may have to jump out of windows, or use drugs which are difficult to obtain and of the specific effects of which they are not fully informed. Physicians and other experts, who do know the proper combination and quantities of drugs needed, usually refuse help, either because of moral objections or in fear of legal liabilities. They impose their own socially supported moral beliefs on patients who do not share them, but cannot act unaided. Dr. Jack Kevorkian is a rare and courageous exception.

To be sure, compassionate physicians may feel that terminal patients in extreme pain should be helped to end such pain. They may discreetly prescribe anesthetics which end suffering by ending life. There have been no successful prosecutions for this quasi-legal practice, although some unsuccessful ones have been brought and physicians who prescribe painkillers in the required quantities assume some risk. Physicians also may withhold life-prolonging treatment at the directions of patients or of legal guardians. Patients do have a legal right to refuse any treatment—though the extent of that right is not well defined. However, merely withholding treatment still may lead to an unnecessarily prolonged, stressful, and perhaps painful way of dying.

WHO SHOULD DECIDE?

Even physicians such as Dr. Kevorkian, willing to take major legal risks, have helped only patients who were incurable and, in most cases, had reached a terminal stage. This takes the decision on whether to end life out of the hands of a mentally competent patient and places it into the hands of a physician, who must decide that the patient is terminal enough, or has suffered enough, before helping him to die. He may also refuse to help at all.

Giving physicians (or any other persons) the authority to veto a patient's decision seems unwarranted. Physicians are trained in how to treat diseases so as to prolong life. They are not experts on whether or not to prolong it. There is no training for making such a decision. Indeed, physicians are taught (*primum non laedere* [first, do no harm]) always to prolong life. No respect is instilled for the patient's wishes, if he prefers to shorten his life. Yet, whether and when to end a person's life is a moral, not a medical, decision, for the patient to make, not the doctor. The physician's task is to inform the patient of his prognosis, perhaps to advise him, and, above all, to help him carry out his decision.

Imagine a 20-year-old patient hospitalized for a condition which, although incurable, is neither terminal nor acutely painful. In the patient's rational, carefully considered view his condition denies him the pleasures of life. He wants to die, but needs assistance. Since he is neither terminal nor suffering unbearable pain, most physicians would be unwilling to help and would run a major legal risk if they did. Again, imagine a 90-year-old who feels that life is of no further interest to him, although he is neither terminal nor in pain. He too will find it hard to persuade a physician to help him die if he cannot do so by himself.

SUICIDE AND THE DISABLED

For good or bad reasons, people commit suicide every day. Since many would-be suicides act on impulses which may turn out to be temporary, forcing a moderate delay seems in their interest and legitimate—but is not to be confused with preclusion. Imagine now a healthy young man who, perhaps influenced by Arthur Schopenhauer's philosophy [best known for its pessimism], has decided to commit suicide. Before he has a chance to kill himself, a traffic accident leaves him paralyzed and hospitalized, incurable but not terminal. He now has additional reasons to end his life but is less able, perhaps altogether unable, to do so unless aided. Although we do not make it easy, we cannot prevent an able person from ending his life anytime he wants to. But we can prevent a disabled person from doing the same. Thus we add to the disability nature or accident has inflicted.

A RIGHT TO DIE

If the law is to respect fundamental rights, it must not inquire into the why and how of suicide. Just as the right to property entails the right to give it away or destroy it, the right to live entails the right to die. The decision of whether to commit or assist a suicide should remain with the individual.

Jacob Sullum, *Reason*, May 1991.

This seems odd because our compassionate society usually goes out of its way to help the disabled overcome whatever handicaps are in the way of their desires. Employers are legally compelled to hire disabled persons, schools to make special arrangements to teach them. Public buildings and transportation are made accessible to the wheelchair-bound. Yet, when it comes to suicide, we refuse to allow any assistance to the disabled. We exploit their disability to prevent them from doing what able-bodied persons can do. On all other occasions we try to compensate for the disadvantages nature inflicts on some. Yet when assistance is essential to enable the disabled to commit suicide, we threaten to prosecute anyone who helps them.

Despite the receding influence of religious ideas and our official unwillingness to impose them, and despite the precariousness of the notion that society has a compelling interest in preventing suicide, we continue to treat life as a social duty that individuals, however disabled, should not be helped to shirk. It is not clear to whom the duty to live could be owed. Once the government no longer legally recognizes God as the authority to which duties are owed, nature cannot have prescriptive authority to force unwilling persons to live, since such authority would have to come from God. Only society is left as the source of this alleged duty. But society cannot be shown to have a compelling interest in forcing persons to live against their will. Moreover, such an interest would hardly justify the cruelty involved. To be sure, the great majority has an instinctive wish to live. But why should we enforce the gratification of this wish on those who, for whatever reason, decide not to gratify it?

ASSESSING MENTAL COMPETENCE

Since, from a secular viewpoint, the moral right to die can hardly be less fundamental than the moral right to live, our non-recognition of the former must flow from unacknowledged residual theological notions which we have officially renounced imposing on non-believers. Dimly realizing as much, most persons opposed to assistance in suicide tend to avoid moral arguments in favor of prudential arguments. These are of two kinds. The first questions the mental competence of individuals who want to hasten their death. The second questions the disinterestedness of persons willing to help them. We must also deal with questions about ending the life of persons who are in a terminal phase of disease, but not mentally competent to make decisions, and of persons in a permanent coma. These are particularly sticky questions, since ending the life of these two classes of patients would be homicide, justifiable or not, rather than suicide, since, by definition, the patients do not make the decision themselves.

How can we assess the mental competence of a physically disabled person who decides on suicide? The task is daunting but not impossible. First of all, prejudicial notions must be discarded. A patient who wants his life ended need not be mentally sick, clinically depressed, or temporarily deranged. The idea that he must be mentally sick merely justifies a conclusion foreordained by circular reasoning. Having discarded prejudicial notions, psychiatrists, using their customary methods, can ascertain whether the patient knows who and where he is, and whether his mental processes are realistic and logical to the normal degree. A conversation about what led to his decision is apposite as well. Reasonable opponents of suicide, religious or not, may be invited to participate where feasible. (The whole process could be videotaped if the patient's competence is controversial.) Beyond the judgment of the psychiatrist, based on these data, nothing is needed. The patient's decision should be accepted.

Intellectual competence is to be investigated, not what is sometimes referred to as emotional health. "Emotional health" is not a clinical concept, but a moral concept quite amorphous and subject to fashion. It allows the imposition of moral views on a patient who may be diagnosed as emotionally ill if he does not share them.

SAFEGUARDS

How can we make sure that no one will be pressed to end his or her life by self-interested relatives, friends, enemies, or caretakers? What about undue influence? Safeguards have long been developed to make sure that a patient's decisions about his last will are uncontaminated. These safeguards can be used as well to ensure that his decision about assisted suicide is independent. Where there are problems with the medical prognosis on which the patient's decision may depend, these must be dealt with by means of second or third opinions.

As for the terminal patient who is incompetent or unconscious, if he has provided instructions while competent, they should be followed. If he has not, the decision of relatives and legal guardians must be followed, unless there is evidence to make them suspect. If the situation is cloudy (or if the patient has no relatives) the hospital could name someone, preferably a physician familiar with the patient's syndrome, but practicing elsewhere, to make the decision. If his prognosis and decision agree with those of the treating physician there is no problem. If not, the two physicians will have to ask a third physician willing to decide within 36 hours. Decisions should be independent of the views of hospital administrators and allow ending life when there is no chance of regaining consciousness.

ASSISTED SUICIDE AND ABORTION

Sometimes an analogy between assisted suicide and abortion is suggested. Indeed, opponents of one usually oppose the other as well; in both cases the opposition may ultimately rest on traditional religious ideas even if the opponents are not religious. But the analogy is misleading. Abortion destroys a fetus with the consent of the mother and usually reflects her interests. The fetus does not make the decision and cannot be consulted. Conceivably the fetus could have an interest in survival. If allowed to develop, the fetus may be expected to desire and enjoy life. In contrast, assisted suicide shortens the life of a patient who has decided himself that prolongation does not serve his interests. Surely, the normal fetus could not be assumed to have an interest in self-destruction. The suicidal patient does. (Conflicts about abortion usually are about alleged fetal v. alleged maternal rights, with some denying fetal rights. But no one would deny that suicide patients are persons who have rights.)

THE "SLIPPERY SLOPE" ARGUMENT

Most arguments about assisted suicide can be dealt with in a reasonable, if not perfect, way. However, the "slippery slope" argument, though influential, is hard to deal with rationally. It suggests that, once we allow doctors to shorten the life of patients who request it, doctors could and would wantonly kill burdensome patients who do not want to die. This suggestion is not justified. The specter of Nazi practices is usually raised to make it credible. But Nazi practices were imposed on physicians and hospitals by political directives which did not evolve from any prior authority given physicians to assist in suicide. There was no "slippery slope." Nor can it be found elsewhere in medical practice. Physicians often prescribe drugs which, in doses greater than prescribed, would kill the patient. No one fears that the actual doses prescribed will lead to the use of lethal doses. No one objects to such prescriptions in fear of a "slippery slope." The "slippery slope" idea seems fortunately to be an unrealistic nightmare. Authorizing physicians to assist in shortening the life of patients who request this assistance no more implies authority to shorten the life of patients who want to prolong it, than authority for surgery to remove the gall bladder implies authority to remove the patient's heart.

> "People possess a dignity to which rights attach that not even they have the moral authority to waive, i.e., inalienable rights."

SUICIDE IS NOT AN INDIVIDUAL RIGHT

Robert P. George and William C. Porth Jr.

In the following viewpoint, Robert P. George and William C. Porth Jr. refute Ernest van den Haag's argument in the preceding viewpoint that individuals have a right to commit suicide. George and Porth contend that the right to life is fundamental and inalienable. Moreover, the authors maintain, a human being cannot be owned, not even by oneself; therefore, they argue, individuals do not have the right to kill themselves. George is a lawyer who teaches legal and political theory at Princeton University in New Jersey. Porth is a lawyer and writer.

As you read, consider the following questions:

1. What reasons do the authors give to support their contention that people cannot be owned?
2. If society recognizes the right to assisted suicide, who should help with such suicides, according to George and Porth?
3. What evidence do the authors present to support their contention that society is already sliding down "the slippery slope"?

From Robert P. George and William C. Porth Jr., "Death, Be Not Proud," *National Review*, June 26, 1995; ©1995 by National Review, Inc., 215 Lexington Ave., New York, NY 10016. Reprinted by permission.

D arwin had his Huxley. [Thomas Henry Huxley was one of the first scientists to accept and defend Charles Darwin's theory of evolution.] Dr. Jack Kevorkian has at long last found his in the person of Professor Ernest van den Haag. In the June 12, 1995, issue of the *National Review*, Professor van den Haag champions not only a legal right to commit suicide, but a right to demand medical assistance in doing so, praising Kevorkian as a "rare and courageous exception" to the refusal of most doctors to extend such "help." Granted that Dr. Kevorkian at least manifests the courage of his convictions, are we ready to embrace his vision not only as an acceptable medical ethic but as the basis for a new legal entitlement that would play its part in shaping the future of American society? Van den Haag is clearly ready, but the rest of us would do well to reflect a little more carefully on the implications of a sweeping right to death.

According to van den Haag, our failure to recognize a legal right to suicide is a remnant of the sway of Christianity over Western society. He even asserts that, before Christianity, governments were "unconcerned with suicide," deeming it either expedient or honorable. As in the analogous case of the wildly inaccurate historical account of abortion law given by Justice Harry A. Blackmun in *Roe v. Wade*, bad history paves the way for bad political philosophy and deplorable law.

An Abominable Act

Suicide has been condemned and proscribed in a wide array of societies throughout history. To cite only a couple of instances predating the birth of Christ, suicide has always stood under a general condemnation in Jewish law, and Aristotle, in Book V of *Nicomachean Ethics*, addresses why the state punishes a man who kills himself (not merely why the state *should* punish him, it must be stressed, but why it in fact *does*). The philosophical rejection of suicide has also been widespread, although not universal, and it has only sometimes been dependent on the precepts of revealed religion, Christian or otherwise. As the German philosopher Immanuel Kant observed, "Suicide is not abominable because God forbids it; God forbids it because it is abominable." Are millennia of law, tradition, and moral reasoning as undeserving of regard and as easily dismissed as Professor van den Haag imagines?

Even the foundational instrument of American democracy would have to go. According to the Declaration of Independence, each of us is endowed by our Creator with certain inalienable rights, including, notably, the right to life. Ought

Americans to continue to credit this teaching? We can't if we accept van den Haag's notion of a freely alienable right to life, under which people would have the right to kill themselves and, indeed, to authorize others to kill them. "From a secular viewpoint," he declares, "the moral right to die can hardly be less fundamental than the moral right to live." So much for the inalienable right to life.

THE CREATOR'S ROLE

What of the Declaration's acknowledgment of the role of the "Creator"? Van den Haag makes short work of Him by denying the legitimacy of legislating on the basis of religiously informed moral judgments. He treats the inalienability of the right to life as nothing more than an "unacknowledged residual theological notion which we have officially renounced imposing on non-believers." This same stricture, he argues, eliminates even natural-law arguments against suicide: "Once the government no longer recognizes God as the authority to which duties are owed, nature cannot have prescriptive authority to force unwilling persons to live, since it would have to come from God."

Here, of course, van den Haag courts self-defeat. Natural law is not some oppressive external edict. It is the product of human reason directed to the eternal question of what it means to flourish fully as human beings. Such moral reasoning is foundational to any consideration of human rights. Either van den Haag's argument undercuts all moral claims, including his own claim of a moral right to commit suicide, or it proves nothing. If he is prepared to embrace moral subjectivism or relativism as a consequence of what he takes to be our "renunciation" of imposing "theological notions" on non-believers, then he has no basis for arguing that society does anything wrong in imposing its views on non-believers or violating what he takes to be people's moral rights, including their alleged moral right to kill themselves. But if he eschews subjectivism and relativism, then he will need to adduce some ground of moral rights which survives his own strictures against appealing to divine or natural law. Moral libertarians have been pushing this boulder up the hill for a long time now; it keeps rolling back and crushing them.

In any event, to van den Haag it "seems irrefutable, if religion is disregarded," that people have a right to kill themselves. His intellectual case for this alleged "right to die" is simple: 1) people own themselves; 2) owners can dispose of their property as they see fit; 3) people are therefore entitled to kill themselves, and even to engage the help of others in doing so.

CAN PEOPLE BE OWNED?

Van den Haag's argument for the notoriously controversial proposition that individuals "own themselves" is that "without God (or slavery) no one else really could." Astonishingly, in view of its prominence in philosophical literature, the possibility seems not to have occurred to him that people are "owned" neither by themselves, nor by other people, nor (in any sense analogous to the human ownership of property) by God. People simply are not owned by anyone; nor, in any morally permissible way, can they be owned.

As subjects of moral rights and obligations, people are not chattels to be owned, traded, or disposed of as they or anyone else "sees fit." As *persons*, not merely *things*, human beings have intrinsic, not merely instrumental, value. Hence people possess a dignity to which rights attach that not even they have the moral authority to waive, i.e., *inalienable* rights.

In defending a right to commit suicide, van den Haag makes an implicit appeal to J.S. Mill's principle that people ought to be free to do as they please so long as they do not directly harm others. Mill himself, however, saw that his "harm principle" could not rationally be stretched to authorize people to "dispose of themselves as they see fit." For example, he famously denied that people have a moral right to sell themselves into slavery. Whatever is ultimately to be said for and against his philosophy of liberty, Mill stands with Thomas Jefferson, not van den Haag, on the question of inalienable rights.

Van den Haag's uncritical appeal to the idea of self-ownership renders his argument utterly unpersuasive. In fact, if people are the sorts of things that can be "owned" and "disposed of" as the owner "sees fit," then it is difficult to imagine what grounds could be given for believing that people have *moral* rights at all. And if people have no moral rights, then they cannot have what van den Haag calls the moral right to die. To treat the right to life as anything but inalienable ultimately undercuts all claims to moral rights.

Moreover, any theory of self-ownership, even one such as John Locke's (which is far less imperialistic than van den Haag's), will have to identify the source of one's property interest in oneself. Mere "possession" cannot be enough. That provides no one with a morally compelling reason to refrain from, for example, seizing another and making him a slave. Obviously van den Haag cannot claim that God grants us title to ourselves; nor can he maintain that it derives from nature. Watch out, Professor, here comes that boulder!

The long and short of the matter is that van den Haag's argument for a moral right to die is anything but "irrefutable." It leaves untouched the most telling and—truth be told—the most obvious counterarguments, and rests on premises that eviscerate the moral force of the conclusions they are designed to support.

The shaky ground on which Professor van den Haag constructs his right to suicide becomes no stabler when he moves to the right to assistance in committing suicide. Here he contends that physicians who refuse to honor their patients' requests for help in killing themselves "impose their own socially supported moral beliefs on patients who do not share them, but cannot act unaided." Such a physician, according to van den Haag, exercises a "veto" over the patient's decision. And "giving physicians (or any other person) the authority to veto a patient's decision seems unwarranted."

So, in the Brave New World of Professor van den Haag, doctors who dissent from the new moral orthodoxy are guilty of imposing their morality on others simply by declining to do what they believe is morally wrong. What would a moral libertarian propose for dealing with people who insist on imposing their morality on others? Fines? License suspension or revocation? Some even more severe sanction? Whatever the solution, it would presumably take the form of some species of coercion designed to force dissenting physicians to get with the moral-libertarian program.

A DUTY TO PROMOTE LIFE

To be fair, van den Haag does not stipulate that he would *require* doctors to assist in suicides. But his argument tends nowhere else, since he maintains that it is a violation of a patient's rights to withhold such assistance. Obviously, though, government compulsion of doctors to assist in suicides could only result in the vindication of one putative moral right (that of a patient to kill himself) at the direct expense of another (that of a doctor to refrain from performing or facilitating such a killing). We therefore face the high irony that the assisted-suicide agenda diminishes the humanity of both patients and doctors: the former by treating their lives as disposable things; the latter, by treating them as mere instruments to carry out the wishes of their patients.

Part of van den Haag's error is his conception of the doctor's role. He sees it as essentially catering to the patient's desires. But there is no more reason to suppose that a doctor has a duty to gratify a patient's desire for death than that he has a duty to gratify his desire for the euphoria of addictive drugs. Physicians pledge themselves to promote human life and health. They have no right to *compel* a patient to act in service of those ends. But they themselves have a duty not to act against them. And they have a duty not to act except in accordance with their own expertise and professional judgment. Thus, a doctor should not infect a patient with a disease or amputate a healthy limb simply because an eccentric patient desires it. And if he should not do the lesser wrong of intentionally harming a patient's bodily well-being, he should not do the greater wrong of intentionally destroying a patient's life.

ONLY GOD CAN DECIDE

In the end, law cannot really resolve the complexities of a situation that involves religion, ethics, medicine and what people think of the ultimate mystery of human existence. Amid all the clamor and confusion, Catholics and other persons of faith should proclaim quietly and without arrogance or dogmatism that God is the author of all human life. Only God has the right to determine the time of its termination.

Robert F. Drinan, *America*, June 4, 1994.

Curiously, van den Haag does not expressly discuss why he hits upon doctors as the persons whom society should select to carry out the task of assisting would-be suicides. Certainly physicians possess a comprehensive knowledge of the vulnerabilities of human bodies. But one does not need all the training of an engineer to be a saboteur or the skill of an anatomist to be a butcher. Indeed, there is something more than faintly unsettling about asking the preservers of life to play so prominent a role in destroying it, much as if a government bent on iconoclasm insisted that painters and sculptors take the lead in smashing the images on which they had labored. If society decides to recognize a right of assisted suicide, the simplest way of implementing it might be to expand the duties of the mortician. He is already adept at using the syringe to withdraw and inject fluids. With a modicum of additional training he could administer a fatal injection and then have the body right at hand for his customary ministrations. The efficiencies of such a scheme are obvious, and even the title of "mortician" seems singularly apt.

As a further argument, van den Haag proposes that failure to provide assistance in committing suicide "discriminates" against those who, because of paralysis or some other disability, cannot destroy themselves unaided. This is a truly bizarre notion. Simply because government cannot prevent some people from transgressing its laws does not require it to assist others in doing so. The same is true of such harmful and even immoral conduct as government prudently declines to criminalize. For example, an ordinary adult may choose to drink himself into oblivion in the privacy of his home; but it does not follow that we discriminate against a quadriplegic who may be similarly inclined when the government does not provide him with a helper to purchase and ply him with alcohol.

NEXT STEPS?

Professor van den Haag's final effort is to rebut prudential concerns which might make a society wary of legalizing assisted suicide, even if it were persuaded of its theoretical justification. Such concerns are legion, but van den Haag addresses only a few. These fall into four basic categories: difficulties in ensuring the mental competence of a would-be suicide, necessary safeguards against undue influence being used to persuade someone to accept being killed, the need for substituted decision-making for the unconscious and the incompetent, and the fear that acceptance of assisted suicide will lead to worse things.

The question of mental competence van den Haag would handle by empowering psychiatrists, "using their customary methods," to rule upon the sanity of a person who elects to have himself killed. But there is no need to keep the process simple; so he suggests that "reasonable opponents of suicide, religious or not, may be invited to participate," and the "whole process" may be videotaped in controversial cases. Although van den Haag does not discuss the prospect, when two or more psychiatrists disagree, one must assume that the whole circus would end up before the courts, even if the mechanism for the competency hearing was such that it did not begin there. Isn't that an attractive prospect to add to the dockets of a medico-legal system already filled with acrimony and overloaded to the breaking point?

With respect to the fear of undue influence, van den Haag is far less specific. He assures us that "safeguards have long been developed to make sure that a patient's decisions about his last will are uncontaminated" and these "can be used as well to ensure that his decision about assisted suicide is independent." Yet he doesn't indicate what safeguards he may have in mind. Since the chief safeguard against undue influence upon testators is the right to challenge their wills during the probate process, this particular safeguard might come a little late for the weak and elderly relative who has been overzealously persuaded to call for the lethal injection. The only timely safeguard would seem to be another pre-suicide hearing, at which a different set of experts and lawyers could explore the possibility of undue influence.

Perhaps we are too pessimistic about the proliferation of these hearings. Since there is a tendency for many professional services to gravitate to where they can be adequately compensated, maybe these proceedings would reach full flower only when a Mellon or a Rockefeller contemplated ending it all. In the case of the middle class, and especially the poor, it may be that these hearings would be perfunctory, if not absent altogether. Many "unimportant" people might pass through the hands of the suicide facilitators in a brisk and efficient fashion. Alas, this prospect offers us strangely little reassurance.

DETERMINING AN ACCEPTABLE MARGIN FOR ERROR

Van den Haag's third prudential concern is the need for a proper mechanism for substituted decision-making, so that the mentally impaired and the comatose will not be denied the benefits of assisted suicide. Such a mechanism would not be a novelty in American society. Since the withholding of nutrition and hydration has been allowed to be directed by relatives in many instances under the guise of declining "medical treatment" (see "Killing Grounds," *National Review*, March 6, 1995), one could say that we already have experience with one strain of third-party election of assisted suicide. The results are not encouraging. Apart from the moral objections to allowing someone to decide to have someone else killed, the number of cases in which our medical experts have proved to be wrong in their predictions is alarming. Professor van den Haag assures us that he would allow third-party election of assisted suicide only when there is no chance of a patient regaining consciousness. The problem is that medical science seems incapable of making this judgment with anything even remotely approaching accuracy. As Wesley J. Smith reported in the aforementioned article, one study published in 1991 in the *Archives of Neurology* found that 58 per cent of patients with a "firm diagnosis" of being in a persistent vegetative state recovered consciousness within three years. Of course, such embarrassing statistics might tend to disappear if we were to embrace surrogate decision-making for assisted suicide, but this wouldn't mean that the errors would cease, only our painful consciousness of them. In this area, what would be an acceptable incidence of error? One per cent? One-tenth of one per cent? What would be a tolerable sacrifice for this questionable moral "progress"?

A LOGICAL PROGRESSION

This brings us to a final area of prudential concern and the question perhaps most worth pondering: What sort of society would creation of a right to assisted suicide help us to become? Professor van den Haag is curtly dismissive of the notion that it would be likely to lead to moral deterioration and a slide from acceptance of suicide as a "rational" and legitimate choice to acceptance of "mercy killing" with or without the victim's consent and even to the disposal of those who desire to cling to life but whose desire is deemed selfish or irrational. But the slope becomes very slippery very fast as soon as a society begins acting on the proposition that some people are better off dead. We cannot forget that legalizing suicide means legitimizing the taking of an innocent human life, albeit one's own. And once a society has acknowledged as reasonable that there can be lives not worth living, and therefore rightly eliminated, only sentimentality stands in the way of embracing the concept of "*lebensunwertes Leben*"—"life unworthy of life."

We are well into our slide. Consider the widespread approval, discussed above, of depriving comatose patients of food and water. Consider recent proposals from the highest ranks of the American medical profession to allow harvesting of organs from anencephalic infants *before death*. Consider the even more "advanced" state of affairs in the Netherlands, where non-consensual euthanasia is common. Does all this appear to be anything but a perfectly logical progression? It is but a short step from judging that a person who is old, infirm, and in pain can rationally "choose death" to concluding that it is irrational for such a person to refuse to make that choice. As our population ages, government will face increased burdens in caring for the elderly. It is not unrealistic to fear that government may assume what began as a private prerogative, and move from making life-and-death decisions for the comatose, to making them for the insane, for the retarded, for those of less-than-average intelligence, and finally for those who are entirely rational and intelligent, but whose desire to cling to life brands them as obstinate, uncooperative, and just plain unreasonable. Are we then to rely on nothing but the heroism of individual doctors to restrain the abuses of government? If so, let us hope there are some "rare and courageous exceptions" among physicians of a rather different stripe from Dr. Jack Kevorkian.

| *"What interest can the state possibly have in requiring the prolongation of a life that is all but ended?"*

ASSISTED SUICIDE IS A CONSTITUTIONAL RIGHT

Roger Miner

In July 1994, physician Timothy E. Quill and two other doctors unsuccessfully challenged the constitutionality of New York State's prohibitions against assisted suicide. They appealed the decision in that case, and in *Quill v. Vacco*, Roger Miner, a circuit judge for the U.S. Court of Appeals for the Second Circuit, ruled in their favor. The following viewpoint is excerpted from Miner's decision, in which he asserts that the ban against assisted suicide is unconstitutional because it violates the Fourteenth Amendment's equal protection clause. Under the ban, he writes, patients who are on life-support systems may legally hasten their death by turning off the machines, but terminally ill patients who are not on life support do not have that option. Such a distinction between the two classes of patients is unconstitutional, he rules.

As you read, consider the following questions:

1. According to the author, why is the removal of life-support systems not a natural means of death?
2. How is writing a prescription to hasten death a less active role for a physician than disconnecting life-support systems, in Miner's opinion?
3. What regulations may the state of New York require for physician-assisted suicide, according to the author?

From Roger Miner's decision in *Quill v. Vacco*, no. 95-7028, April 2, 1996.

The action giving rise to this appeal was commenced by a complaint filed on July 20, 1994. The plaintiffs named in that complaint were the three physicians who are the appellants here and three individuals then in the final stages of terminal illness: Jane Doe (who chose to conceal her actual identity), George A. Kingsley and William A. Barth. The sole defendant named in that complaint was G. Oliver Koppell, then the Attorney General of the State of New York. He has been succeeded as Attorney General by Dennis C. Vacco, who has been substituted for him as an appellee on this appeal. According to the complaint, Jane Doe was a 76-year-old retired physical education instructor who was dying of thyroid cancer; Mr. Kingsley was a 48-year-old publishing executive suffering from AIDS; and Mr. Barth was a 28-year-old former fashion editor under treatment for AIDS. Each of these plaintiffs alleged that she or he had been advised and understood that she or he was in the terminal stage of a terminal illness and that there was no chance of recovery. Each sought to hasten death "in a certain and humane manner" and for that purpose sought "necessary medical assistance in the form of medications prescribed by [her or his] physician to be self-administered."

CHALLENGES TO THE NEW YORK PENAL LAW

The physician plaintiffs alleged that they encountered, in the course of their medical practices, "mentally competent, terminally ill patients who request assistance in the voluntary self-termination of life." Many of these patients apparently "experience chronic, intractable pain and/or intolerable suffering" and seek to hasten their deaths for those reasons. Mr. Barth was one of the patients who sought the assistance of Dr. Grossman. Each of the physician plaintiffs has alleged that "[u]nder certain circumstances it would be consistent with the standards of [his] medical practice" to assist in hastening death by prescribing drugs for patients to self-administer for that purpose. The physicians alleged that they were unable to exercise their best professional judgment to prescribe the requested drugs, and the other plaintiffs alleged that they were unable to receive the requested drugs, because of the prohibitions contained in sections 125.15(3) and 120.30 of the New York Penal Law, all plaintiffs being residents of New York.

Section 125.15 of the New York Penal Law provides in pertinent part: "A person is guilty of manslaughter in the second degree when: . . . 3. He intentionally . . . aids another person to commit suicide." A violation of this provision is classified as a class C felony.

Section 120.30 of the New York Penal Law provides: "A person is guilty of promoting a suicide attempt when he intentionally . . . aids another person to attempt suicide." A violation of this provision is classified as a class E felony.

Count I of the complaint included an allegation that "[t]he Fourteenth Amendment guarantees the liberty of mentally competent, terminally ill adults with no chance of recovery to make decisions about the end of their lives." It also included an allegation that

[t]he Fourteenth Amendment guarantees the liberty of physicians to practice medicine consistent with their best professional judgment, including using their skills and powers to facilitate the exercise of the decision of competent, terminally ill adults to hasten inevitable death by prescribing suitable medications for the patient to self-administer for that purpose.

Count II of the complaint included an allegation that

[t]he relevant portions of . . . the New York Penal Law deny the patient-plaintiffs and the patients of the physician-plaintiffs the equal protection of the law by denying them the right to choose to hasten inevitable death, while terminally ill persons whose treatment includes life support are able to exercise this choice with necessary medical assistance by directing termination of such treatment.

In their prayer for relief the plaintiffs requested judgment declaring the New York statutes complained of constitutionally invalid. . . . Plaintiffs also sought an order permanently enjoining defendants from enforcing the statutes and an award of attorney's fees. . . .

THE RIGHT TO REFUSE MEDICAL TREATMENT

The right to refuse medical treatment long has been recognized in New York. In 1914 Judge Benjamin Cardozo wrote that, under New York law, "[e]very human being of adult years and sound mind has a right to determine what shall be done with his own body." In 1981, the New York Court of Appeals held in In re Eichner that this right extended to the withdrawal of life-support systems. The Eichner case involved a terminally-ill, 83-year-old patient whose guardian ultimately was authorized to withdraw the patient's respirator. The Court of Appeals determined that the guardian had proved by clear and convincing evidence that the patient, prior to becoming incompetent due to illness, had consistently expressed his view that life should not be prolonged if there was no hope of recovery. In In re Storar, the companion case to Eichner, the Court of Appeals determined that a profoundly retarded, terminally-ill patient was incapable of making a decision to terminate blood transfusions. There, the patient was incapable of making a reasoned decision, having never been competent at any time in his life. In both these cases, the New York Court of Appeals recognized the right of a competent, terminally-ill patient to hasten his death upon proper proof of his desire to do so.

SUPPORT FOR A CONSTITUTIONAL RIGHT

The essence of the substantive component of the Due Process Clause is to limit the ability of the state to intrude into most important matters of our lives, at least without substantial justification. In a long line of cases, the Supreme Court has carved out certain key moments and decisions in individuals' lives and placed them beyond the general prohibitory authority of the state. The Court has recognized that the Fourteenth Amendment affords constitutional protection to personal decisions relating to marriage, *Loving v. Virginia* (1967), procreation, *Skinner v. Oklahoma* (1942), family relationships, *Prince v. Massachusetts* (1944), child rearing and education, *Pierce v. Society of Sisters* (1925), and intercourse for purposes other than procreation, *Griswold v. Connecticut* (1965). The Court has recognized the right of individuals to be free from government interference in deciding matters as personal as whether to bear or beget a child, *Eisenstadt v. Baird* (1972), and whether to continue an unwanted pregnancy to term, *Roe v. Wade* (1973).

A common thread running through these cases is that they involve decisions that are highly personal and intimate, as well as of great importance to the individual. Certainly, few decisions are more personal, intimate or important than the decision to end one's life, especially when the reason for doing so is to avoid excessive and protracted pain. Accordingly, we believe the cases from *Pierce* through *Roe* provide strong general support for our conclusion that a liberty interest in controlling the time and manner of one's death is protected by the Due Process Clause of the Fourteenth Amendment.

James R. Browning et al., *Compassion in Dying v. State of Washington*, March 6, 1996.

The Court of Appeals revisited the issue in *Rivers v. Katz* (1986) (establishing the right of mentally incompetent persons to refuse certain drugs). In that case, the Court recognized the right to bring on death by refusing medical treatment not only as a "fundamental common-law right" but also as "coextensive with [a] patient's liberty interest protected by the due process clause of our State Constitution." The following language was included in the opinion:

> In our system of a free government, where notions of individual autonomy and free choice are cherished, it is the individual who must have the final say in respect to decisions regarding his medical treatment in order to insure that the greatest possible protection is accorded his autonomy and freedom from unwanted interference with the furtherance of his own desires.

After these cases were decided, the New York legislature placed its imprimatur upon the right of competent citizens to hasten death by refusing medical treatment and by directing physicians to remove life-support systems already in place. In 1987, the legislature enacted Article 29-B of the New York Public Health Law, entitled "Orders Not to Resuscitate." The Article provides that an "adult with capacity" may direct the issuance of an order not to resuscitate. . . .

In 1990, the New York legislature enacted Article 29-C of the Public Health Law, entitled "Health Care Agents and Proxies." This statute allows for a person to sign a health care proxy for the purpose of appointing an agent with "authority to make any and all health care decisions on the principal's behalf that the principal could make.". . . Accordingly, a patient has the right to hasten death by empowering an agent to require a physician to withdraw life-support systems. . . .

UNEQUAL TREATMENT

In view of the foregoing, it seems clear that New York does not treat similarly circumstanced persons alike: those in the final stages of terminal illness who are on life-support systems are allowed to hasten their deaths by directing the removal of such systems; but those who are similarly situated, except for the previous attachment of life-sustaining equipment, are not allowed to hasten death by self-administering prescribed drugs. The district judge in Quill v. Vacco has identified "a difference between allowing nature to take its course, even in the most severe situations, and intentionally using an artificial death-producing device." But Justice Antonin Scalia, for one, has remarked upon "the irrelevance of the action-inaction distinction," noting that "the cause of death in both cases is the suicide's conscious decision to 'pu[t] an end to his own existence.'". . .

Indeed, there is nothing "natural" about causing death by means other than the original illness or its complications. The withdrawal of nutrition brings on death by starvation, the withdrawal of hydration brings on death by dehydration, and the withdrawal of ventilation brings about respiratory failure. By ordering the discontinuance of these artificial life-sustaining processes or refusing to accept them in the first place, a patient hastens his death by means that are not natural in any sense. It certainly cannot be said that the death that immediately ensues is the natural result of the progression of the disease or condition from which the patient suffers.

IT IS ABOUT FREEDOM

The right to be let alone.

That is what the physician-assisted suicide issue and the man who has pioneered and personalized it, Dr. Jack Kevorkian, are really all about: freedom. This is not about the "right to die." (Like it or not, we are all going to die anyway.)

What this is all about is personal autonomy. About denying that the state has any right to compel innocent, competent adults to needlessly suffer. How can anyone who wants less government interference in his life *not* also demand the right to be free of state interference in the most intimate and personal decision of all?

Jack Lessenberry, *World & I*, April 1994.

Moreover, the writing of a prescription to hasten death, after consultation with a patient, involves a far less active role for the physician than is required in bringing about death through asphyxiation, starvation and/or dehydration. Withdrawal of life support requires physicians or those acting at their direction physically to remove equipment and, often, to administer palliative drugs which may themselves contribute to death. The ending of life by these means is nothing more nor less than assisted suicide. It simply cannot be said that those mentally competent, terminally-ill persons who seek to hasten death but whose treatment does not include life support are treated equally.

AN IRRATIONAL INTEREST

A finding of unequal treatment does not, of course, end the inquiry, unless it is determined that the inequality is not rationally related to some legitimate state interest. The burden is upon the plaintiffs to demonstrate irrationality. At oral argument and in its brief, the state's contention in *Quill v. Vacco* has been that its principal interest is in preserving the life of all its citizens at all times and under all conditions. But what interest can the state possibly have in requiring the prolongation of a life that is all but ended? Surely, the state's interest lessens as the potential for life diminishes. And what business is it of the state to require the continuation of agony when the result is imminent and inevitable? What concern prompts the state to interfere with a mentally competent patient's "right to define [his] own concept of existence, of meaning, of the universe, and of the mystery of human life," as the Supreme Court wrote in 1992 in *Planned Parenthood v. Casey*, when the patient seeks to have drugs prescribed to end life during the final stages of a terminal illness? The greatly reduced interest of the state in preserving life compels the answer to these questions: "None."

A three-judge panel of the Ninth Circuit Court of Appeals attempted to identify some state interests in reversing a district court decision holding unconstitutional a statute of the state of Washington criminalizing the promotion of a suicide attempt in *Compassion in Dying v. Washington*. The plaintiffs in the Washington case contended for physician-assisted suicide for the terminally-ill, but the panel majority found that the statute prohibiting suicide promotion furthered the following: the interest in denying to physicians "the role of killers of their patients"; the interest in avoiding psychological pressure upon the elderly and infirm to consent to death; the interest of preventing the exploitation of the poor and minorities; the interest in protecting handicapped persons against societal indifference; the interest in preventing the sort of abuse that "has occurred in the Netherlands where . . . legal guidelines have tacitly allowed assisted suicide or euthanasia in response to a repeated request from a suffering, competent patient." The panel majority also raised a question relative to the lack of clear definition of the term "terminally ill." [An eleven-judge panel of the Ninth Circuit Court of Appeals reviewed and reversed the decision of the three-judge panel in March 1996.]

No State Interests Are Served

The New York statutes prohibiting assisted suicide, which are similar to the Washington statute, do not serve any of the state interests noted, in view of the statutory and common law schemes allowing suicide through the withdrawal of life-sustaining treatment. Physicians do not fulfill the role of "killer" by prescribing drugs to hasten death any more than they do by disconnecting life-support systems. Likewise, "psychological pressure" can be applied just as much upon the elderly and infirm to consent to withdrawal of life-sustaining equipment as to take drugs to hasten death. There is no clear indication that there has been any problem in regard to the former, and there should be none as to the latter. In any event, the state of New York may establish rules and procedures to assure that all choices are free of such pressures. With respect to the protection of minorities, the poor and the non–mentally handicapped, it suffices to say that these classes of persons are entitled to treatment equal to that afforded to all those who now may hasten death by means of life-support withdrawal. In point of fact, these persons *themselves* are entitled to hasten death by requesting such withdrawal and should be free to do so by requesting appropriate medication to terminate life during the final stages of terminal illness.

As to the interest in avoiding abuse similar to that occurring in the Netherlands, it seems clear that some physicians there practice nonvoluntary euthanasia, although it is not legal to do so. The plaintiffs here do not argue for euthanasia at all but for assisted suicide for terminally-ill, mentally competent patients, who would self-administer the lethal drugs. It is difficult to see how the relief the plaintiffs seek would lead to the abuses found in the Netherlands. Moreover, note should be taken of the fact that the Royal Dutch Medical Association recently adopted new guidelines for those physicians who choose to accede to the wishes of patients to hasten death. Under the new guidelines, patients must self-administer drugs whenever possible, and physicians must obtain a second opinion from another physician who has no relationship with the requesting physician or his patient.

Finally, it seems clear that most physicians would agree on the definition of "terminally ill," at least for the purpose of the relief that plaintiffs seek. The plaintiffs seek to hasten death only where a patient is in the "final stages" of "terminal illness," and it seems even more certain that physicians would agree on when this condition occurs. Physicians are accustomed to advising patients and their families in this regard and frequently do so when decisions are to be made regarding the furnishing or withdrawal of life-support systems. Again, New York may define that stage of illness with greater particularity, require the opinion of more than one physician or impose any other obligation upon patients and physicians who collaborate in hastening death.

Equal Protection Is Violated

The New York statutes criminalizing assisted suicide violate the Equal Protection Clause because, to the extent that they prohibit a physician from prescribing medications to be self-administered by a mentally competent, terminally-ill person in the final stages of his terminal illness, they are not rationally related to any legitimate state interest.

VIEWPOINT

| "Mentally competent, terminally ill adults do not have a fundamental right to commit physician-assisted suicide."

ASSISTED SUICIDE IS NOT A CONSTITUTIONAL RIGHT

Robert R. Beezer

Robert R. Beezer is a circuit judge for the U.S. Court of Appeals for the Ninth Circuit in San Francisco. The following viewpoint is taken from Beezer's dissenting opinion in *Compassion in Dying v. State of Washington*, in which the right-to-die group Compassion in Dying challenged Washington's laws against assisted suicide on behalf of three terminally ill patients and their physician. Beezer argues that laws prohibiting assisted suicide are not unconstitutional because there is no fundamental right to assisted suicide. Patients on life-support systems who seek to hasten their death by refusing treatment are not in the same legal class as terminally ill patients who seek physician-assisted suicide, Beezer contends. Furthermore, he maintains that the state's interests in preserving life outweigh any individual liberty to commit suicide.

As you read, consider the following questions:

1. What are the four interests the state of Washington recognizes in end-of-life cases, according to the author?
2. How do patients on life support differ from terminally ill patients who seek physician-assisted suicide, in Beezer's opinion?
3. What question concerning physician-assisted suicide should the courts decide, in the author's view?

From Robert R. Beezer's dissenting opinion in the decision of *Compassion in Dying v. State of Washington*, no. 94-35534, March 6, 1996.

Plaintiffs [in *Compassion in Dying v. State of Washington*] allege that RCW 9A.36.060 [Washington's law prohibiting assisted suicide] violates their substantive due process rights under the Fourteenth Amendment of the United States Constitution. They argue that physician-assisted suicide fits within the broad description of the liberty aspect of the substantive due process right set forth in *Planned Parenthood v. Casey*:

> These matters, including the most intimate and personal choices a person may make in a lifetime, choices central to personal dignity and autonomy, are central to the liberty protected by the Fourteenth Amendment. At the heart of liberty is the right to define one's own concept of existence, of meaning, of the universe, and of the mystery of human life.

A Liberty Interest

Specifically, plaintiffs allege that mentally competent, terminally ill adults have a constitutionally protected liberty interest in committing physician-assisted suicide. . . .

I would hold that mentally competent, terminally ill adults do not have a fundamental right to commit physician-assisted suicide. The Supreme Court has repeatedly indicated an unwillingness to expand the list of rights deemed fundamental. Physician-assisted suicide is not currently on that list. To be fundamental, a liberty interest must be central to personal autonomy or deeply rooted in history. The district court relies on language in *Casey's* plurality opinion to hold that substantive due process protects a wide range of autonomy-based liberty interests, including physician-assisted suicide. Such a reading of *Casey* is permissible, provided it is clearly understood that the liberty interests so protected are not fundamental. *Casey's* reaffirmation of the abortion right is best understood as a decision that relies heavily on stare decisis [precedent]; the abortion right, uniquely protected under the undue burden standard, is sui generis [in a class by itself]. The second test for determining the existence of fundamental rights, whether the interest is rooted in the nation's history, similarly militates against a fundamental right to physician-assisted suicide.

No New Fundamental Rights

While the list of fundamental rights has not been definitively closed to expansion, the Supreme Court has indicated an unwillingness to find new penumbral, privacy-type fundamental rights. In *Reno v. Flores* (1993), the Court refuses to expand the list of fundamental rights to include a right of juveniles to be released into a noncustodial setting. Reno states:

> We are unaware . . . that any court—aside from the courts be-
> low—has ever held that [the asserted fundamental right exists].
> The mere novelty of such a claim is reason enough to doubt that
> "substantive due process" sustains it; the alleged right certainly
> cannot be considered "'so rooted in the traditions and con-
> science of our people as to be ranked as fundamental.'". . .

What Right to Die?

The judicial discovery of a sweeping constitutional right to die is
analytically unconvincing and politically indefensible. The recent
decisions [*Compassion in Dying v. Washington* and *Quill v. Vacco*] rely
heavily on the similarities between abortion and euthanasia,
both of which, to use Ronald Dworkin's typically abstract for-
mulation, involve "choices for death." Both euthanasia and abortion inspire profound religious and moral disputes; both have
been, at certain times in American history, prohibited by the
states; and the case for each becomes more or less compelling at
different points in the life cycle. But creating constitutional
rights by analogy is often treacherous, as the Supreme Court discovered in the wake of *Roe v. Wade*, when it was witheringly criti-
cized for expanding its earlier cases concerning the privacy of
the marital bedroom into an apparently unrelated right of doctors to perform first-trimester abortions in hospitals. By blithely
repeating the errors of *Roe*, and expanding the narrow right to
refuse unwanted medical treatment into a much broader right to
hasten one's own death, the recent assisted suicide decisions
show the dangers of constitutional abstraction.

Jeffrey Rosen, *New Republic*, June 24, 1996.

The sweeping description of liberty in *Casey* is never characterized as "fundamental" under the Constitution; rather, its wide
purview covers all liberty protected by the Fourteenth Amendment, nonfundamental as well as fundamental.

There is no fundamental liberty interest in physician-assisted
suicide. First, there is no history or tradition supporting any
form of suicide. Second, however compelling the suicidal
wishes of terminally ill patients are regarded, it cannot honestly
be said that neither liberty nor justice will exist if access to
physician-assisted suicide is proscribed. . . .

The State's Interests

Whatever test is ultimately used to evaluate the constitutionality
of RCW 9A.36.060, the plaintiffs' liberty interest must be com-

pared against the state interests underlying the statute.

The State asserts three interests: (1) preventing suicide, (2) protecting vulnerable individuals from abuse or undue influence and (3) preserving and protecting the lives of its people. It asserts that the interest in preventing suicide applies equally to all the state's citizens; the State does not evaluate the quality of life among its citizenry, and preserve and protect only those whose lives are deemed "worth living."

Washington courts recognize four state interests common to end-of-life cases: (1) the preservation of life, (2) the protection of the interests of innocent third parties, (3) the prevention of suicide, and (4) the maintenance of the ethical integrity of the medical profession. The Supreme Court has also recognized all four of these state interests.

The four governmental interests recognized by Washington courts and endorsed by the Supreme Court are all very strong, and apply with undiminished vigor to justify RCW 9A.36.060's prohibition of physician-assisted suicide for mentally competent, terminally ill adults. Any one of these interests would be sufficient to support this application of the statute under a rational relationship test. Were it necessary for me to do so, I would even be inclined to hold that the cumulative force of all four governmental interests is sufficient to enable this application of the statute to withstand strict scrutiny. . . .

The Rational Relationship Test

In reviewing a statute's constitutionality under the substantive due process clause, courts should apply one of two tests. If the right asserted is fundamental, the statute is subjected to strict scrutiny, under which it must be narrowly tailored to serve a compelling state interest. If the liberty interest is not fundamental, the statute is subjected only to the "unexacting" inquiry of whether the statute rationally advances some legitimate governmental purpose.

Because I would hold that the liberty interest of mentally competent, terminally ill adults in committing physician-assisted suicide is not a fundamental right, I would use the latter test, which has sometimes been called the rational relationship test.

The nonfundamental liberty interest at stake here is the right of mentally competent, terminally ill adults to commit physician-assisted suicide. This interest is rooted in the liberty to make intensely private choices that are central to personal dignity and autonomy. The exercise of this nonfundamental liberty interest is barred in Washington by RCW 9A.36.060, which states that promoting a suicide attempt is a criminal offense. The Washington statute rationally advances four legitimate state interests: the preservation of life, the protection of the interests of innocent third parties, the prevention of suicide, and the maintenance of the ethical integrity of the medical profession. Under the rational relationship test, RCW 9A.36.060 is valid.

The district court also holds that the Washington statute violates the Equal Protection Clause. Its analysis is based upon two premises, both of which are incorrect, and fall together. First, it assumes that Cruzan-type patients [those who need life-support systems to stay alive] are similarly situated to the patients in this case. Second, it holds that the differentiation between these types of patients is subject to, and does not withstand, strict scrutiny.

A RADICAL DEPARTURE

For the 2nd Circuit to declare who may be charged with a homicide in New York and under what circumstances is a radical departure from the proper judicial role. A declaration by a court that assistance in self-destruction is a "benefit" or "right" for one particular class of citizens, while remaining a crime when inflicted upon all other citizens, would be tantamount to deciding that some persons are truly better off dead than alive. How such a mandate could be rooted in the Constitution defies reasoned explanation. Our Constitution does not mandate that state-licensed healing professionals be permitted to assist in the self-destruction of any class of citizens.

U.S. Catholic Conference et al., *Origins*, December 12, 1996.

Cruzan-type patients are being subjected to unwanted life-saving medical treatment, from which they have a constitutionally protected right to be free. The patients in this case, though also terminally ill, are not seeking any such freedom from treatment. Rather, they are seeking medical assistance in ending their lives. The district court rejected arguments that the distinction between the two groups is one between "natural" and "artificial" deaths. There are dozens of ways that the two groups of patients could be distinguished or associated, not the least of which is the dramatic difference in the nature of their constitutional rights. One group has not just an interest but a right to be free from unwanted medical treatment. The other group has an interest, but not a protected right, in committing physician-assisted suicide. Washington statutes clearly distinguish the two groups, as does the AMA Code of Ethics. They are not similarly situated, and are therefore not subject to an equal protection analysis.

Even though the physician plaintiffs argue that the two groups are similarly situated, the patients in this case are neither a suspect classification nor holders of fundamental rights. The patients' position is entitled to no more than rational basis review. Strict scrutiny is only used where people are categorized into suspect classifications (e.g., race) or suffer the infringement of a constitutionally protected fundamental right. According to the U.S. Supreme Court in *Schweiker v. Wilson*, "[T]he pertinent inquiry is whether the [classification] advances legitimate legislative goals in a rational fashion. The Court has said that, although this rational basis standard is 'not a toothless one,' it does not allow us to substitute our notions of good public policy." The state's interests in protecting life, preventing suicide, protecting the interests of third parties, and preserving the ethical integrity of the medical profession are strong, perhaps even compelling. Even if the two groups—patients refusing unwanted medical treatment and mentally competent terminally ill adults seeking to commit physician-assisted suicide—were similarly situated, the distinction between them rests solidly on a rational basis and is constitutionally valid under the Equal Protection Clause.

A MORAL ISSUE

The issue of whether mentally competent, terminally ill adults have a constitutionally protected right to commit physician-assisted suicide is one of the most difficult, divisive and heart-wrenching issues facing the courts today. The correlative issue of whether terminally ill loved ones ought to be allowed to commit assisted suicide is likewise one of the most difficult, divisive and heart-wrenching issues facing American society. The former is a constitutional issue for the courts; the latter is a moral question for society as a whole.

The two issues are not the same. The latter requires us—all of us, not just judges—to engage in a soul-searching dialogue about our collective morals. Given the tremendous advances in twentieth-century medical technology and public health, it is now possible to live much longer than at any time in recorded history. We have controlled most of the swift and merciful diseases that caused most deaths in the past. In their place are a host of diseases that cause a slow deterioration of the human condition: cancer, Alzheimer's disease, and AIDS are but a few. This change has forced us to step back and reexamine the historic presumption that all human lives are equally and intrinsically valuable. Viewed most charitably, this reexamination may be interpreted as our struggle with the question whether we as a society are willing to excuse the terminally ill for deciding that their lives are no longer worth living. Viewed less charitably, the reexamination may be interpreted as a mere rationalization for housecleaning, cost-cutting and burden-shifting—a way to get rid of those whose lives we deem worthless. Whether the charitable or uncharitable characterization ultimately prevails is a question that must be resolved by the people through deliberative decisionmaking in the voting booth, as in Washington in 1991, California in 1992 and Oregon in 1994, or in the legislatures, as recently undertaken in Michigan and New York. This issue we, the courts, need not—and should not—decide.

A USURPATION OF STATES' RIGHTS

Instead, we should restrict our decision to the former issue: whether mentally competent, terminally ill adults have a constitutionally protected liberty interest in committing physician-assisted suicide. This is the first federal appellate case in our nation's history to address the issue of physician-assisted suicide. To declare a constitutional right to physician-assisted suicide would be to impose upon the nation a repeal of local laws. Such a declaration would also usurp states' rights to regulate and further the practice of medicine, insofar as a right to physician-assisted suicide flies in the face of well-established state laws governing the medical profession. Finally, the rationales under which we are asked to create this right fail adequately to distinguish physician-assisted suicide as a unique category. If physician-assisted suicide for mentally competent, terminally ill adults is made a constitutional right, voluntary euthanasia for weaker patients, unable to self-terminate, will soon follow. After voluntary euthanasia, it is but a short step to a "substituted judgment" or "best interests" analysis for terminally ill patients who have not yet expressed their constitutionally sanctioned desire to be dispatched from this world. This is the sure and inevitable path, as the Dutch experience has amply demonstrated. It is not a path I would start down.

I would hold that the four state interests are sufficiently strong to sustain the constitutionality of RCW 9A.36.060 as applied to plaintiffs' asserted liberty interest.

I dissent.

PERIODICAL BIBLIOGRAPHY

The following articles have been selected to supplement the diverse views presented in this chapter. Addresses are provided for periodicals not indexed in the *Readers' Guide to Periodical Literature*, the *Alternative Press Index*, the *Social Sciences Index*, or the *Index to Legal Periodicals and Books*.

Peter J. Bernardi	"The Hidden Engines of the Suicide Rights Movement," *America*, May 6, 1995.
Dudley Clendinen	"When Death Is a Blessing and Life Is Not," *New York Times*, February 5, 1996.
Robert F. Drinan	"The Law and Assisted Suicide," *America*, June 4, 1994.
Nina George Hacker	"Death on Demand," *Family Voice*, June 1996. Available from Concerned Women for America, 370 L'Enfant Promenade SW, Suite 800, Washington, DC 20024.
Jason A. Lief	"Constitution Provides No Right to Be Killed," *National Law Journal*, August 26, 1996. Available from 345 Park Ave. South, New York, NY 10010.
Thomas A. Preston	"Killing Pain, Ending Life," *New York Times*, November 1, 1994.
Jeffrey Rosen	"What Right to Die?" *New Republic*, June 24, 1996.
Susan Schindehette and Gail Wescott	"Deciding Not to Die," *People Weekly*, January 18, 1993.
Andrew Solomon	"A Death of One's Own," *New Yorker*, May 22, 1995.
Phyllis Taylor	"Dying with Dignity," *Sojourners*, August 1994.
Ernest van den Haag	"Duty to Live?" *National Review*, April 8, 1996.
Brian Young	"Is Death a Constitutional Right? The Sanctity of Life," *World & I*, April 1994.

WHAT ARE THE CAUSES OF TEEN SUICIDE?

CHAPTER PREFACE

The number of adolescents and young adults who kill themselves has soared since the 1950s, making suicide the third leading cause of death for those aged fifteen to twenty-four. Suicide rates for fifteen- to nineteen-year-olds have quadrupled since the 1950s. Counselors and sociologists are especially concerned about the suicide rate for black youth. Statistics show that the suicide rate for blacks aged fifteen to twenty-four increased by 63 percent between 1980 and 1993, while the rate for white youths in the same age group increased by only 8 percent. The surge in the black male suicide rate is closing the gap between the rates for white and black males. The suicide rate for fifteen- to twenty-four-year-old black males rose from 12.3 per 100,000 in 1980 to 20.1 per 100,000 in 1993. By comparison, the suicide rate for white males in the same age group was relatively flat during the same period: 21.4 per 100,000 in 1980 to 23.1 per 100,000 in 1993. The Centers for Disease Control and Prevention predicts that if the trend continues "suicide rates for young African-Americans will [soon exceed] those of whites."

Suicide experts are puzzled by the rapid increase in the black male suicide rate. Some researchers argue that the cause does not seem to be entirely racial; the suicide rate of black females has changed little during the same period and has even declined in certain age groups. Some social scientists theorize that as blacks achieve greater parity with whites, they acquire some of the same problems as well, resulting in a similar suicide rate for young males of both races. Other researchers believe the surge in black male suicide rates is related to the social ills—such as substance abuse and poverty—that trouble the black community. Whatever the cause, most agree that the ready availability of firearms is an important factor in the rising suicide rate of blacks as well as whites, as most of the increase in suicides during the 1980s involved guns.

While it is difficult to ascertain exactly what causes are fueling the rising teenage suicide rate, social scientists and suicidologists agree that many factors can contribute to an individual teenager's decision to commit suicide. Possible factors include drug and alcohol abuse, mental illness, stress, and a death or other disruption in the family. The authors in the following chapter discuss some of these factors and other possible causes of teen suicide.

"By restricting teen-agers' access to guns, suicides among adolescents could be reduced by 20 percent."

GUNS IN THE HOME CONTRIBUTE TO TEEN SUICIDE

Christopher Scanlan

In the following viewpoint, Christopher Scanlan asserts that the easy availability of guns contributes to the high rate of teen suicide. Scanlan maintains that the suicide rate of teenagers who kill themselves with firearms has increased dramatically while suicides by other means have remained the same. Teen suicide rates would drop significantly if teenagers' access to guns was restricted, he contends. Scanlan is a reporter in the Washington bureau of Knight-Ridder News Service.

As you read, consider the following questions:

1. According to Scanlan, how many youths between the ages of ten and nineteen kill themselves with guns every year?
2. What percentage of adolescents killed themselves with firearms in 1990, according to the author?
3. What evidence does Scanlan present to support the contention that the availability of firearms increases the risk of suicide?

Reprinted from Christopher Scanlan, "Adolescent Angst, a Loaded Gun Are a Fatal Combination," *St. Paul Pioneer Press*, June 27, 1993, with permission of Knight-Ridder/ Tribune Information Services.

In the basement of his Lemont, Ill., home, 14-year-old Paul Hoffman puts the barrel of a .22-caliber rifle under his chin and pulls the trigger. The gun had been kept in his parents' bedroom closet. Paul's last words: "My father doesn't love me."

In rural Philadelphia, Miss., a 16-year-old girl shoots herself in the head after an argument with her boyfriend. She got the gun from her mother's car. In suburban San Diego, Calif., a 15-year-old girl runs into her parents' bedroom after fighting with her mother. Minutes later, a shot rings out.

"I didn't think she knew where the gun was," her grief-stricken father said. "I didn't think she knew where I hid the bullets. I didn't think she knew we even had a gun."

A FATAL COMBINATION

Adolescent angst and a loaded gun. In a nation where half the homes contain at least one firearm, it's a fatal combination that annually kills more than 1,400 American youths between the ages of 10 and 19: one every six hours.

Alarmed by rising teen suicide rates, a growing number of suicide prevention experts, grieving parents and gun owners want to focus attention on a prevention strategy that both sides in the volatile gun debate can agree on: saving kids from themselves by keeping guns out of their reach.

The most optimistic advocates predict that by restricting teen-agers' access to guns, suicides among adolescents could be reduced by 20 percent. That's nearly 300 teen-agers a year.

"This is an area where we may be able to rise above the ideological mire that we've been stuck in for so long," said Dr. James Mercy, acting head of the Violence Prevention Division of the National Center for Injury Prevention and Control.

Teen suicide rates have quadrupled since 1950, federal statistics show. A panel of leading firearm researchers concluded in 1992 that the increase was fueled by rapid growth in gun suicides, noting that hangings and other nonfirearm suicides had remained essentially unchanged since the 1930s.

An equally disturbing trend of self-inflicted deaths has surfaced among younger children, according to a 1993 report. Between 1979 and 1988, the suicide rate among children between the ages of 10 and 14 jumped 75 percent, the highest rate increase for all youth age groups, the Centers for Disease Control and Prevention reported in June 1993.

Overall in 1990, there were 2,237 suicides among 10- to 19-year-olds, according to the latest figures from the National Center for Health Statistics.

Nearly two-thirds—142 children between 10 and 14 and 1,332 teen-agers between 15 and 19—killed themselves with a gun.

Guns also put at risk large numbers of young people who consider suicide. A 1990 nationwide federal health survey of high school students found that more than one in four had thought seriously about attempting suicide. Sixteen percent made a specific plan to commit suicide; of those, about half tried—and needed medical attention.

TEEN SUICIDE AND GUN CONTROL

But teen suicides often go unnoticed in the contentious national debate over firearm violence and gun control. "It's a piece of the firearms story that has not been told," said Lois Fingerhut, an epidemiologist for the National Center for Health Statistics who has published several studies analyzing firearm deaths among children, teens and young adults.

In a nationwide survey of youth suicide prevention programs in September 1992, none reported a major effort to limit gun access. And government resources are being targeted at other problems: $10 million to fight violence against women and $6 million to prevent homicide and other interpersonal violence against young people.

One hopeful sign: In April 1993, the American Association of Suicidology, the largest organization of suicide professionals, voted to organize a workshop to bring together health advocates and gun enthusiasts "to seek common ground on the issue of reducing unsupervised access to firearms among our nation's youth."

"Sounds good to me. We're here and waiting," said Paul Blackman, research coordinator for the National Rifle Association.

Still, the National Rifle Association is skeptical. The organization notes that the suicidology group sides with gun control advocates in favoring laws that restrict gun access.

Blackman and a handful of other researchers don't think banning handguns is the answer. A study by a University of Washington researcher compared the overall suicide rates in Canada and the United States. Brandon Centerwall found that although handgun availability in the United States was 10 times greater, the Canadian suicide rate was 13 percent higher. Gun control critics say Japan, too, has very low rates of gun ownership, but has suicide rates as high or higher than in the United States.

But the CDC and most suicide researchers say there is more compelling evidence to suggest the availability of firearms increases the risk of suicide.

A 1991 study in western Pennsylvania found that the risk of youth suicide increases when guns are present in the home, no matter how carefully they are stored.

MORE GUNS LEAD TO MORE GUN SUICIDES

In the past decade, physicians and public health workers have been documenting the relatedness between the easy availability of guns and suicide. . . .

This and other research refutes the routinely heard argument of inevitability: those who are suicidal will do it one way or the other. Studies certify the opposite: that the increase in guns—from 54 million in 1950 to more than 200 million in 1989—coincides with a rise in firearm suicides. The latter rose 20 percent between 1980 and 1991.

The strongest increase has been among the young, typically a group given to impulses and opting for quick solutions to life's difficulties. A 1991 American Medical Association study reported that teenagers in a home with a gun overwhelmingly chose that method to kill themselves, while those in gunless homes rarely used firearms as a means of death.

Colman McCarthy, *Liberal Opinion Week*, April 24, 1995.

And a study published in May 1993 by the same team found that a loaded gun in the home poses a serious risk even when a teen is not mentally ill. "We used to say if you have a kid who's suicidal or psychiatrically ill, get the guns out of the home. Now our point is that it seems as if guns pose a hazard for suicide no matter what risk category you're in," said the author, Dr. David Brent of the University of Pittsburgh.

AN ENDURING PROBLEM

No one expects to prevent all or even most of the child and teen suicides reported every year. Suicide among all ages remains one of the nation's most enduring public health problems. And guns are a method rather than a cause for an act that suicide experts describe as infinitely complex in its motives.

"We're always talking about a 12 or 15 or 30 variable equation," agrees David C. Clark, director of the Center for Suicide Research and Prevention in Chicago.

"We're trying to pick out single variables in the string that we might be able to attack in the hope that if we remove that one element, that one brick from the wall, the whole wall will come tumbling down. I think (reducing access to guns) is a brick, and I think the rates will drop."

Said Mercy: "Without ready access to guns, many youth suicides might remain suicide attempts." Unlike elderly suicides who seem more likely to have a "clear and sustained intent" to kill themselves, "young people . . . are impulsive and not particularly skilled in communication," he and two other CDC researchers said in a 1991 editorial in the *Journal of the American Medical Association*.

Think back to your own teen-age years, suicide experts advise parents who have guns and adolescents at home.

"If your girlfriend belittles you at the mall, there's just no reason to live. If your parents treat you badly, it's like the worst disaster on Earth that you can never overcome. But the next morning you've forgotten it because something else neat happened," said Patrick O'Carroll, former chief of the CDC's intentional injury section.

"Gun control is not an effective way to reduce suicide."

THE NUMBER OF GUN-RELATED TEEN SUICIDES IS EXAGGERATED

David B. Kopel

Many gun-control advocates assert that removing firearms from the home would reduce the rate of teen suicide. In the following viewpoint, David B. Kopel contends that gun-control advocates have exaggerated the extent of teen suicide by firearms. Kopel argues that while the percentage of teen suicide by firearms is high in the United States, the numbers have remained stable for many years. However, he maintains, teen suicides have increased dramatically in other countries where guns are much more difficult to obtain. If guns are not available, teenagers who want to kill themselves will merely find another method, he claims. Kopel is the author of several books on gun control.

As you read, consider the following questions:

1. According to Kopel, what facts must be changed to make this statement true: "Every three hours, a teenager commits suicide with a handgun"?
2. What factors that might affect suicide did Gary Kleck take into account in his analysis, according to Kopel?
3. How much more likely is it for a teenager who lives in a home with a gun to commit suicide than one who lives in a home without a gun, according to the author?

Reprinted from David B. Kopel, "Gun Play," with permission, from the July 1993 issue of *Reason* magazine. Copyright 1993 by the Reason Foundation, 3415 S. Sepulveda Blvd., Suite 400, Los Angeles, CA 90034.

Gun suicides account for the deaths of many young people—more than 2,000 in 1990. From the mid-1950s to the late '70s, teenage suicide rose sharply, and most of the increase was due to gun suicides. But since then, the teenage suicide rate has remained stable, and so has the percentage of suicides involving guns. Teenagers are still less likely to commit suicide than any older age group.

FALSE STATISTICS

Although the teenage suicide rate has been about the same since the late '70s, gun-control advocates insist that immediate action is necessary to address this "crisis." They often cite false statistics to justify their sense of urgency. In 1989, for example, the American Academy of Pediatrics told a congressional committee that "every three hours, a teenager commits suicide with a handgun." But this figure is valid only if one counts all suicides as handgun suicides, or if one calls every person under 25 a teenager.

In addition to exaggerating the extent of the problem, gun-control supporters simply assume that fewer firearms would mean fewer suicides. One might speculate that the presence of a gun can turn a teenager's fleeting impulse into an irrevocable decision. If guns were less readily available, perhaps suicide would decline. This theory is intuitively plausible, but it is not consistent with the evidence.

GUN-CONTROL LAWS HAVE NO EFFECT

In his 1991 book *Point Blank*, Florida State University criminologist Gary Kleck analyzes suicide rates and gun laws in every American city with a population over 100,000. He takes into account all the factors that might affect suicide, such as race (whites are more likely to commit suicide), religion (Catholics are less likely), economic circumstances, and 19 gun-control laws, ranging from waiting periods to handgun bans. Kleck finds no evidence that any of the gun-control laws had a statistically significant effect on suicide rates. While some gun-control laws did affect the rate of gun suicide, the total suicide rate remained the same. People who had decided to kill themselves simply substituted other, equally lethal methods.

Data from other countries appear to support Kleck's conclusion that gun control is not an effective way to reduce suicide. While teenage suicide has remained stable in the United States since 1978, it has risen sharply in Europe, where gun control is much stricter. In Great Britain, where gun laws are very strict and the gun ownership rate is less than one-tenth that in the United States, adolescent suicide has risen by more than 25 percent in just five years. Similarly, in Japan handguns and rifles are illegal and shotguns very difficult to obtain. Yet teenage suicide is 30 percent more frequent in Japan than in the United States.

OTHER UNTRUE FACTOIDS

Given the lack of evidence that gun control reduces suicide, anti-gun activists have resorted to factoids such as this one, reported by *Washington Post* columnist Richard Reeves in September 1992: "Teen-agers in homes with guns are 75 times more likely to kill themselves than teen-agers living in homes without guns." The story behind this factoid illustrates how myths that support gun control are generated.

A 1991 article in the *Journal of the American Medical Association* discussed a study of several dozen homes in western Pennsylvania where a teenager had committed or attempted suicide or where a non-suicidal teenager who had been admitted to a psychiatric hospital lived. A home with a teenager who had committed suicide was twice as likely as the other homes to contain a gun. In an editorial accompanying the article, three employees of the federal Centers for Disease Control incorrectly wrote: "The odds that potential suicidal adolescents will kill themselves go up 75-fold when a gun is kept in the home."

CAR EXHAUST, NOT FIREARMS

An issue health advocacy articles stressed during the 1980s [was] the poignant phenomenon of suicide among young males, which was supposed to be increasing because of growing firearms availability. Naturally, no health advocate mentioned that suicide among teenagers and young adults has been increasing in much of the industrialized world. By the same token, readers of health advocacy articles blaming American suicide increases in these groups on guns will never learn: (a) that while suicide among American males aged 15–24 increased 7.4 percent in the period 1980–90, (b) the increase in England for this group was over ten times greater (78 percent), with car exhaust poisoning being used most often.

Don B. Kates et al., *Guns: Who Should Have Them?* David B. Kopel, ed., 1995.

JAMA later published a retraction, noting that the 75-fold figure was incorrect; the increase was in fact twofold (and the number was merely a correlation, not proof of cause). Senator

John Chafee saw the false claim but apparently missed the correction, since he repeated the 75-fold figure in a congressional hearing in October 1992. In his *Washington Post* column, Reeves took the factoid one step further, telling his readers that it applied to all teenagers, even though all of the subjects in the study had serious psychological problems.

"There is no doubt that the existing evidence points to an inordinate risk of suicide facing homosexual and bisexual youth."

HOMOSEXUAL TEENS ARE AT HIGH RISK FOR SUICIDE

Gary Remafedi

In the following viewpoint, Gary Remafedi contends that many studies show a high rate of suicide attempts among gay teenagers. However, he argues, this link between homosexuality and suicide has often been overlooked due to the lack of government support of these studies, the sensitive and controversial subject matter, and the difficulty in determining if suicide victims were homosexual. It is important, Remafedi asserts, that future studies of teen suicide address the issue of homosexuality. Remafedi is the author of several articles on gay youth and suicide. He is also an associate professor of pediatrics and the director of Youth and AIDS Projects at the University of Minnesota.

As you read, consider the following questions:

1. According to Remafedi, by what percentage have teenage suicide rates increased since 1960?
2. Why was the *Report of the Secretary's Task Force on Youth Suicide* almost suppressed, in the author's opinion?
3. What characteristics of gay teens are linked to a high risk of attempted suicide, according to the author?

Taken from Gary Remafedi's "Introduction: The State of Knowledge on Gay, Lesbian, and Bisexual Youth Suicide," in *Death by Denial: Studies of Suicide in Gay and Lesbian Teenagers*, published by Alyson Publications Inc. Copyright ©1994 by Gary Remafedi.

A connection between suicide and homosexuality has long been recognized in the popular culture, reflected in music (e.g., "The Ode to Billie Joe"), movies (e.g., *The Boys in the Band*), theater (e.g., Lillian Hellman's *The Children's Hour*), and other art forms. Yet, few researchers have ventured to explore the link between sexual orientation and self-injury. Early evidence of an association appeared as incidental findings in studies of adult sexuality. They revealed that gay men were much more likely to have attempted suicide than heterosexual men and that their attempts often occurred during adolescence. Newer studies have provided consistent evidence of unusually high rates of attempted suicide among gay youth, in the range of 20–30 percent, regardless of geographic and ethnic variability.

A LEADING KILLER

In the U.S., suicide is the third leading killer of youth, accounting for 14 percent of all deaths in the teen age-range. For uncertain reasons, teenage suicide rates have risen by more than 200 percent since 1960, as compared to a 17 percent increase in the general population. Surveys of youth have found that 6–13 percent of adolescents have attempted suicide at least once in their lives, but only a small percentage of attempters have received appropriate help.

These disturbing observations have led to considerable epidemiological, psychological, medical, and sociological research to understand the epidemic of self-injury and death among youth. However, the unifying characteristics of young victims are still incompletely understood, despite considerable progress and new information. It appears that adolescent suicide victims are a diverse group. While most have discernible psychiatric symptoms, a sizeable minority have not exhibited psychological or behavioral problems before death. Given the many unanswered questions regarding epidemiological trends and causative factors, no stone should be left unturned by scientists exploring the issues.

Unfortunately, the potentially important link between suicide and homosexuality has been overlooked until recent years for a variety of reasons:

1. Governmental agencies have not adequately supported the study of suicide in homosexual populations. Given the events surrounding the [U.S. Department of Health and Human Services'] federally commissioned *Report of the Secretary's Task Force on Youth Suicide*, it appears that political forces were at work to suppress the collection or publication of information which has

been perceived to benefit homosexual communities. The report's controversial chapter on gay and lesbian youth almost led to a rejection of the whole volume. After considerable debate, the report ultimately was accepted in its entirety, but published only in limited edition. . . .

THE TECHNICAL CHALLENGES

2. Another set of impediments to studies of suicide and sexual orientation are the technical challenges. Both are extremely sensitive and controversial subjects, difficult to broach with institutional review boards, professionals, and participants alike. Because adults and, especially, adolescents may keep their sexual orientation hidden, identifying representative samples of gays, lesbians, and bisexuals has been virtually impossible in the climate of American society. Only in the past decade have investigators succeeded in launching research with sizeable samples of gay, lesbian, and bisexual youth, albeit volunteers with unknown biases for participation. Despite the sampling limitations, the works by Stephen G. Schneider et al. and Gary Remafedi et al. are important illustrations of the general feasibility of suicide research with homosexual youth.

These studies also have helped clarify that the risk of attempted suicide is not uniformly distributed among homosexual youth, but linked to particular characteristics. Some characteristics resemble familiar risk factors in the general adolescent population, such as family dysfunction, substance abuse, and sexual abuse. Others are unique to studies of gay and bisexual youth: gender atypicality, young age at the time of gay identity formation, intrapersonal conflict regarding sexuality, and nondisclosure of orientation to others. Although derived from homosexual youth, these data regarding predictions of attempted suicide might help scientists understand other populations as well. For example, the observed relationship between gender nonconformity and attempted suicide may be relevant to any adolescent group, regardless of sexual orientation. . . .

A PAUCITY OF INFORMATION

3. A final, noteworthy barrier to the recognition of the risk for suicide among homosexual youth has been the paucity of information about the sexual orientation of actual suicide victims. Only a small percentage of attempters ultimately will die at their own hands. Suicide attempts are 50–200 times more common than completed suicides. Suicide completers may be a unique subset of all attempters, and data derived from attempters may

not be generalizable to those persons who will someday succeed.

In the *Report of the Secretary's Task Force*, Paul Gibson projected that gay and lesbian youth may account for 30 percent of all youth suicides, based on existing data about the prevalence of homosexuality and the relative risk of attempted suicide. Although this alarming and hotly contested figure may indeed be accurate, it will be important for future studies to gather empirical evidence from the psychological autopsies of adolescent suicide victims. In this type of study, health care records, personal documents, and interviews with friends and family members are used retrospectively to reconstruct the circumstances contributing to a suicide death.

Reprinted by permission of Kirk Anderson.

In lieu of psychological autopsies, the existing information on attempted suicide for gay youth reflects grave potential for lethality. From Ronald F.C. Kourany, we learn that two-thirds of randomly sampled U.S. psychiatrists believed that the self-injurious acts of homosexual adolescents were more serious and lethal than those of heterosexual youth. Moreover, the attempts that my colleagues and I studied were characterized by moderate to high lethality and inaccessibility to rescue in 54 percent and 62 percent of cases, respectively.

To my knowledge, the only psychological autopsy study to examine the sexual orientation of victims systematically has been the work of Charles L. Rich et al. The investigators set out to determine the orientation of adult suicide victims in San

Diego County during a specified time frame in the pre-AIDS era. That 10 percent of suicide victims were found to be gay men is impressive, since the proportion of openly gay men in the U.S. is now thought to be less than 10 percent of males. Moreover, since suicide attempts in homosexual persons have been found to be associated with nondisclosure of orientation, it is reasonable to expect that the 10 percent figure is the lowest possible estimate of the actual proportion of gay suicides in the San Diego cohort. Unfortunately, the authors minimized their own findings by overestimating the prevalence of homosexuality in the general population and underestimating the likelihood of missed cases of gay and lesbian suicide.

THE FUTURE OF RESEARCH

What lies ahead in the future of research and suicide prevention programs for homosexual youth? From the perspective of research design, studies of suicide attempters should move beyond the use of volunteers. Future population-based surveys of adolescent health should routinely ascertain the sexual orientation of respondents, thereby enabling analyses of suicide risk (as well as any number of other health problems) in relation to sexual orientation within respective cohorts of youth. However, even with this improved sampling strategy, investigators will continue to wrestle with the validity of self-reported sexual orientation and the generalizability of findings to youth who cannot disclose their feelings honestly.

It is imperative that future psychological autopsies of adolescent victims address the issue of sexual orientation. Surely, this will require an unprecedented collaboration between suicidologists and sexologists to devise appropriate methods to uncover sensitive sexual information from all available sources at the postmortem. Since gay and lesbian youth who complete suicide may not be "out" to families, it will be important to question friends, teachers, and counselors and to examine other variables which indirectly reflect orientation such as manifest gender role, dating behaviors, pornographic materials, diaries and personal artifacts, telephone records, and other novel strategies.

In the future, investigations of attempted and completed suicide should address the issue of suicide risk for young lesbian women. A retrospective review of records from 500 homosexual youth at the Hetrick-Martin Institute in New York found that female victims of violence reported suicide attempts more often than males (41 percent vs. 34 percent). It remains to be determined whether lesbian status itself is a relative protection or a risk factor for suicide. Both Joseph Harry and I have found gender nonconformity to be a risk for young men. Is it also true of young lesbians, or can we expect the opposite effect? Answering this question may shed new light on the well-recognized, but poorly understood, gender differences in suicidal behavior in the general population. Females attempt suicide at least three times as often as males; but males are approximately four times as likely to die from an attempt (rate of 18.0 per 100,000 vs. 4.4).

IMPORTANT IMPLICATIONS

Beyond academic interest, research pertaining to homosexuality and suicide has important implications for clinical practice and public policy. Completed suicides have been found to be associated with other health problems like substance abuse and HIV/AIDS, all of which are overrepresented in gay communities. Understanding and attacking the root causes of self-injurious behavior in the form of suicide may benefit other community health outcomes, too. From a clinical perspective, neglecting the interrelatedness of risky behavior can adversely affect individual young clients. For example, programs offering HIV-antibody counseling and testing to high-risk adolescents should be mindful of their multiple risks for suicide and proceed with caution. . . .

In my own mind, there is no doubt that the existing evidence points to an inordinate risk of suicide facing homosexual and bisexual youth. Also apparent is the need to expand understanding of the subject. Given what is already known, there is ample reason to earmark research funds for this purpose and to alert human services professionals and students to the current state of knowledge. To ignore the problem now is a missed opportunity to save thousands of young lives, tantamount to sanctioning death by denial.

"Less than one in 10 gay youths attempted suicide because of their homosexuality.... Attempts are always more common than completed suicides."

THE EXTENT OF HOMOSEXUAL TEEN SUICIDE IS EXAGGERATED

Trudy Hutchens

Trudy Hutchens argues in the following viewpoint that gay activists overstate the number of teens who commit suicide because of distress over their sexual orientation. She maintains that many of those gay teens who do kill themselves do so for reasons other than their homosexuality. Although Hutchens states that any suicide is a tragedy, she contends that gay activists are exaggerating the number of homosexual teen suicides in order to gain sympathy and to promote the homosexual lifestyle as normal and healthy. Hutchens is a researcher and writer for *Family Voice*, a monthly periodical published by Concerned Women for America, an organization devoted to promoting traditional Judeo-Christian values.

As you read, consider the following questions:

1. According to Hutchens, why are the statistics cited in Paul Gibson's study skewed?
2. Why is the *Pediatrics* study more reliable than Gibson's study, in the author's opinion?
3. What should Americans who are concerned about teen suicide do, according to Hutchens?

Reprinted from Trudy Hutchens, "Gay Teen Suicide: Myths and Misconceptions," *Family Voice*, August 1996, by permission of the author and Concerned Women for America.

Teen suicide . . . an issue saturated in emotion, grief, and loss. But for homosexual activists it has become a powerful tool to win acceptance in mainstream America. Activists claim gay youths account for almost one-third of all teen suicides—suggesting that society's aversion to homosexuality victimizes gay teens. In other words, we are compelling them to kill themselves. If that is the case, activists conclude, the only way to stop this tragedy is to affirm gay youth. We must embrace and accept their homosexuality as a normal, healthy lifestyle.

The issue of gay teen suicide is part of the homosexual activists' overall game plan. Gay advocates Marshall Kirk and Hunter Madsen outline the strategy in their book *After the Ball*. They urge homosexuals to cast themselves as victims and "invite straights to be their protectors."

A Myth Is Born

The myth of gay teen suicide is largely rooted in a study by Paul Gibson titled "Gay Male and Lesbian Youth Suicide." The study—which claimed that 30 percent of teen suicides are committed by gay youth—was incorporated in a 1989 report published by the Department of Health and Human Services (HHS).

Although homosexual activists managed to get the study included in the government report, then-HHS Secretary Louis Sullivan distanced himself and the department from the study. He wrote, ". . . the views expressed in the paper entitled 'Gay Male and Lesbian Youth Suicide' do not in any way represent my personal beliefs or the beliefs of this department." But by getting the study included in an HHS report, homosexual activists won legitimacy for their cause. When they talked about the tragedy of gay teen suicide, they could then attribute their own skewed statistics to *government sources*.

And skewed they were. First, Gibson harvested his statistics primarily from homosexual sources. Then he applied them to the general population. His claims to validity rested on Dr. Alfred Kinsey's *discredited estimate* that 10 percent of the population is gay. Moreover, the study included statistical impossibilities. For example, Gibson cites an author who stated in the *Washington Blade* (a homosexual newspaper) that as many as 3,000 gay youths commit suicide each year. However, since the *total* teen suicide rate stands at about 2,000 *a year*, Gibson's figures are not only highly exaggerated, but impossible.

Riddled with flaws and false assumptions, Gibson's study also assumes from the outset that homosexuality is natural, inborn, and unchangeable. Despite the countless hours and substantial amounts of money medical researchers have invested trying to prove this proposition, they have yet to produce conclusive evidence.

Even if there were a higher rate of teen suicide among gay youth, a truly fair and unbiased study would acknowledge that other psychological factors could contribute to these suicides.

THE PEDIATRICS STUDY

But while Gibson would not acknowledge these factors, other—more credible—studies have. One study published in *Pediatrics* in 1991, titled "Risk Factors for Attempted Suicide in Gay and Bisexual Youth," evaluated 137 youths who deemed themselves "gay."

Of these 137 teens, 41 (30%) reported a suicide *attempt*. While these statistics may appear to mesh with Gibson's study, it is important to note that Gibson's findings referred to *completed suicides*, not *suicide attempts*—which are always greater in number.

Also worth noting is the fact that 44 percent of those who attempted suicide attributed the cause to "*family problems*." Only one-third of the gay suicide attempters attributed the cause to "personal or interpersonal turmoil regarding homosexuality."

That means that in this study less than one in 10 gay youths *attempted* suicide because of their homosexuality. Again, *attempts* are always more common than *completed suicides*.

A FABRICATED CRISIS

Gay teen suicide is fabricated crisis, the excuse du jour for another binge of social engineering. In 1991, Gallup surveyed teenagers on the leading causes of suicide. Those who said they'd attempted or thought seriously about the act were asked what factors influenced them. Drug and alcohol abuse, grades, family problems and boy-girl relationships all figured prominently. Feelings of anxiety or alienation due to homosexual tendencies didn't even register in the survey.

Don Feder, *Conservative Chronicle*, March 24, 1993.

Dr. David Shaffer, a psychiatrist at Columbia University and a leading expert on teen suicide, explained that Gibson's study "was never subjected to the rigorous peer review that is required for publication in a scientific journal. . . ." In contrast, the study published in *Pediatrics* apparently was subject to such review—and it arrived at a very different conclusion. "In this sample," reported the *Pediatrics* article, "bisexuality or *homosexuality per se was not associated with self-destructive acts.*"

PRO-SEXUAL EDUCATION

Despite the inaccuracies, inconsistencies, and flaws, Gibson's study has become the foundational tool to win acceptance of homosexuality in our nation's public schools. In Massachusetts, Governor William Weld's Commission on Gay and Lesbian Youth cited his findings. The commission used Gibson's study to justify a number of pro-homosexual recommendations, including school-based support groups that affirm homosexuality; gay and lesbian books and resources in the school library; and a curriculum that affirms and promotes the homosexual lifestyle as normal and healthy.

The Sex Information and Education Council of the United States (SIECUS) creates general guidelines for sex education in America's schools. Their guidelines blatantly promote homosexuality even in the earliest grades. According to the 1990 guidelines, children—*ages five through eight*—should be taught that "some men and women are homosexual, which means they will be attracted to and fall in love with someone of the same gender."

In 1992, a school district in Columbia, Maryland, sponsored a one-day seminar on homosexuality and youth. Speakers warned teachers and counselors, "you must affirm a youth's homosexual tendencies, or the teen might commit suicide." They suggested that schools put up posters in the hallway that portray various "families"—such as one made up of two lesbian "mothers."

Speakers urged teachers to keep parents out of the loop. When one teacher asked if she should contact the child's parents about his homosexual feelings, the answer was a resounding "NO!" They explained that many parents would not handle the situation appropriately. And as a result, the child might commit suicide.

"Teen suicide is always a tragedy," noted CWA [Concerned Women for America] Chairman Beverly LaHaye. "But tragedies should never be manipulated in order to advance an agenda—especially one that lures youth into an immoral, disease-ridden lifestyle."

HANDLE WITH PRAYER

Americans concerned about teen suicide should seek out the real causes. We must not become muddled in the myths surrounding the reasons homosexual youth are taking their own lives. And we must remember to take seriously, listen to, and pray for all of America's young people. They are our future.

> "To someone who is profoundly depressed, the option of suicide becomes the only option, the only way to control life and end the unremitting pain."

DEPRESSION CONTRIBUTES TO TEEN SUICIDE

Andrew E. Slaby and Lili Frank Garfinkel

In the following viewpoint, Andrew E. Slaby and Lili Frank Garfinkel contend that an estimated 10 percent of high school students suffer from depression. For many of these teens, the authors maintain, the emotional pain caused by their depression is so debilitating that they begin to believe the only way to ease it is to commit suicide. With proper intervention and treatment, teenagers who are depressed can be helped to overcome their suicidal tendencies, Slaby and Garfinkel assert. Slaby is a psychiatrist in New York specializing in depression and crisis intervention. Garfinkel is a freelance writer.

As you read, consider the following questions:

1. What characteristics must be present for a diagnosis of clinical depression to be made, according to the authors?
2. What are some markers that may predispose teenagers to depression or suicide, according to the authors?
3. In Slaby and Garfinkel's opinion, what is the difference between a suicidal gesture and a suicide attempt?

The current statistics on youth suicide continue to be frightening. More than 5,000 youth under the age of twenty-five kill themselves in the United States every year. Of these, 2,000 are teenagers. And for every completed suicide between 300 and 350 serious attempts are made. Surveys have shown that as many as 60 percent of all high school students have thought about their own death or about killing themselves. In addition, one out of every ten high school students experiences some form of severe depression during the high school years. . . .

THE MENTAL PAIN OF DEPRESSION

Depression is commonly portrayed unidimensionally as profound, all-encompassing sadness. When I ask adults and teens how they would conceptualize a depressed person, they most often describe a hollow-eyed, miserable person who sleepwalks through life before taking an overdose. There is no understanding or recognition of the rage, the fear, and the insurmountable pain that are so much a part of depression. Imagine the worst physical pain you've ever had—a broken bone, a toothache, or labor pain—multiply it tenfold and take away the cause; then you can possibly approximate the pain of depression. The mental pain of depression is so all-consuming that it becomes impossible to derive any pleasure or satisfaction from life; no interests can stimulate attention and perseverance, no persons can adequately foster love or loyalty. The world is seen as bleak and gray. To someone who is profoundly depressed, the option of suicide becomes the only option, the only way to control life and end the unremitting pain.

Depression is a term that has been too loosely integrated into our vocabulary. When we say "I'm so depressed about..." and yet continue to function, work, play, interact with people, it means we're temporarily unhappy about something. Clinical depression, however, is not so transient. A diagnosis of depression is measurable according to specific characteristics, which include sleep disturbance (insomnia or sleeping all the time), changes in eating habits (overeating or lack of appetite), inability to concentrate, physical symptoms (such as headaches, stomachaches), agitation or fatigue, and wretched, morbid thoughts about oneself and the future.

The pain of depression can be far more overwhelming, more incapacitating, than any physical pain. Individuals who are hurting emotionally think poorly of themselves and act in ways that will cause others to think poorly of them. As this cycle is perpetuated, they become more and more isolated and convinced of their worthlessness. It is understandable, then, that persons who are depressed engage in antisocial or delinquent behavior, develop unusually hostile relationships with those closest to them, or experience progressive difficulties with peer relationships. What they are really doing is creating in the minds of others the same negative impressions they already feel about themselves.

Options like reaching out and seeking help are rarely considered or are rejected outright, and as the depression evolves the only option that promises to shut off the pain is suicide.

THE IMPACT OF DEPRESSION

Clinical depression impacts people in real physiological as well as emotional ways. For a diagnosis of clinical depression to be made, it must last at least two weeks and include at least five of the following symptoms: the inability to concentrate, feelings of hopelessness, changes in regular eating habits, sleep disturbances, loss or lack of energy, behavioral changes (restlessness and agitation), engaging in risk-taking behaviors, changes in schoolwork and/or work habits, and thoughts of suicide. Often there is a decrease in sexual energy. In fact, depressed teens may turn to others through sexual encounters in order to gain some acceptance and positive feedback.

It is typical for people with depression to perceive life in an almost totally distorted and negative way, so that thinking and behavior become radically altered. Both one's past history and day-to-day life are rewritten and recast so that everything is seen in the bleakest terms.

It is estimated that approximately one in ten high school students can be diagnosed with depression at some time in his or her life. Many more are never identified. For some fortunate persons, an episode of clinical depression, even untreated, will pass without any lingering effects. For others, therapy and a course of antidepressant medication will be necessary. In either case, most teens who have depression do not go on to attempt or commit suicide. The pressing questions are: Can we determine which kids are more likely to attempt or commit suicide? What separates those people who live with depression from those who are preoccupied with thoughts about suicide, those who make specific plans to kill themselves, or those who actually carry out their plans or impulsively commit suicide?

"Psychological autopsies" of teens who killed themselves or attempted to do so [have] identified those "markers" or features that predispose young people not only to depression but also to suicide. Some of these markers are: a family history of depression or suicide; learning disabilities (primarily because impulsivity is a quality common to both suicide and certain learning disabilities); a history of physical, sexual, or emotional abuse; delinquency; substance abuse; and recurrent, long-lasting episodes of depression.

At some time in our lives we all experience morbid thoughts, thoughts about our own death and the impact our death would have on those around us. Children begin to have these thoughts at an early age, usually around age four, and then again at different times as they mature. Usually these thoughts are transient and not likely to be associated with suicidal behavior. In rare cases, children might be preoccupied with thoughts of death and dying when a grandparent dies, even if a pet dies. They want to join the departed one in heaven. I have interviewed some very young children who have made primitive suicidal gestures for this reason.

Children and teenagers who experience depression at a young age may become dependent on others for affirmation of their very being. Instead of recognizing their own self-worth, they rely on others to provide them with positive feelings. They become needy, dependent, vulnerable teens and adults. Their pathway to help and healing is paved with missed cues and frustration.

ALARMING BEHAVIOR

Young persons who actually formulate a plan for their own suicide may not tell a soul of their plans, or they may swear a single trusted friend to secrecy about their intentions. Some teens even boast in a cavalier or indirect way about how they will one day kill themselves. They may give away treasured possessions; they may write unusually emotional letters to friends or an essay on suicide for English class. These behaviors should be viewed with alarm and clearly warrant immediate counseling and treatment.

When we talk about suicidal gestures, we are referring to attention-seeking behaviors, real cries for help. A suicidal gesture is a deliberate act of self-injury without the intention of dying. Gestures may include ingesting a nonlethal number of pills, self-injury such as minor wrist-slashing, or even waving a firearm around in front of friends. Teens who wave red flags in these ways may not want to die; yet, deaths have been known to occur in spite of the lack of intention.

Suicide attempts are really failed suicides. Some young persons are fortunate enough to be accidentally saved from killing themselves: They are found hanging, but alive, or survive a gunshot wound, or are revived from an overdose. The intent to kill themselves may persist, and they may try again, even succeed. On the other hand, some rescued teens view their survival as a sign that they were not meant to die, and with help they truly begin to work on dealing with their depression.

Any significant crisis related to depression, regardless of how it may manifest itself, should be viewed as a statement about the stresses in a young person's life, a lack of coping mechanisms, and/or society's response to his or her behaviors and problems at that time. The ultimate crisis precipitating the suicide attempt may reflect a breakdown at all three levels: stress and conflict, coping, and societal response.

THE MAJOR CAUSE OF SUICIDE

Depression is a serious, life-threatening illness—the major cause of suicide. Depressive disorders affect an estimated 30 million Americans throughout the socioeconomic spectrum, people of any age, race, religion or education.

Robert H. Gerner, *Los Angeles Times*, August 9, 1993.

Today, depression is better understood than ever before. It is a biological vulnerability that surfaces when sufficiently disturbing life experiences occur. It lies dormant in some individuals only to occur or recur when negative events come to bear on the vulnerable person. Depression alters the individual's functioning, creating additional problems. For instance, lacking the energy or desire to do constructive activities, the depressed teen frequently shows a deterioration in school and social functioning.

Adolescent depression is recognized, diagnosed, and treated more frequently than [ever]. And yet the escalating statistics of adolescent suicide seem to nullify any serious progress. It is ironic that in an age where the cult of youth is so valued, emulated, and pursued, we have been unable to respond to our children and teens when they are in the greatest pain.

This generation of teens will have to learn and integrate—if they haven't already—a whole new system of strategies to cope with the complexity and variety of our societal and cultural norms. Whereas historically the family, the church, and the community frequently provided a safety net for children, where they were nurtured and sheltered and where certain types of behaviors were sanctioned and reinforced, this is no longer the case. Family breakdown, family and community violence, economic instability, stress, drugs—all are far too familiar to teens growing up today. And yet, these are still children, and developmentally they are not ready to face these formidable pressures. Ultimately, the crises that do confront many children who are depressed represent the convergence of complex stressors, immature and ineffectual coping mechanisms, and a lack of societal response.

DID NO ONE SEE THE PAIN?

It is hard to express the pain and poignancy I feel when meeting with families of children who have killed themselves. Whether we meet a week after the suicide or ten years later, I feel connected and bound by the need to help them understand what happened and go on with their lives. I am very aware that, no matter what insight I may help them discover, no matter what resolution or peace they may find in their lives, it will not be enough—they will struggle with guilt and with self-recriminations forever.

In nearly every case of suicide I have reviewed, clues to the adolescent's plans were overlooked or downplayed. They weren't intentionally missed, but unknowingly missed. This does not necessarily mean that the suicide could have been prevented. *Some people will kill themselves no matter what intervention takes place.* In my mind, many adolescent patients remain vulnerable; I worry and wonder how they will respond five or ten years from now, when a crisis may arise and other pressures and circumstances may influence their responses. The histories of many adults who have committed suicide include episodes of severe depression, if not suicide attempts, during adolescence.

Why were the clues missed? Family members and friends did not understand the enormity of the changes they were seeing. They focused on the consequences and not on the underlying problem, so that "family problems" or "drug use" or "anorexia" became the diagnosis. Sometimes the anger, the confusion, and the irritability were treated, but not the depression. The underlying problem remained, torturous and festering. . . .

TREATING DEPRESSION

Among professionals there needs to be a greater understanding of the medical aspect of psychiatric illness that coexists with the psychological forces. Pediatricians, family doctors, internists, and emergency-room physicians must have more intensive training in treating depression. The same energy that we have brought to training students about AIDS and safe sex should be brought to providing knowledge about depression in all its guises. Drug abuse, risk-taking behaviors, promiscuity, and social isolation should provoke questions about suicidal thought and intentions. If we can save more young people it will be worth it.

Suicide is most often the fatal end point of depression, substance abuse, and delinquency. When one sees a pattern that often ends in suicide, immediate attention must be directed to the teen's safety. Hospitalization of the acutely suicidal adolescent is not optional; it cannot be postponed until tomorrow. The young person must be safe, and if the family cannot trust the child over the course of the day and night, then twenty-four-hour care in a hospital is mandatory. If an outpatient level of care is thought to be acceptable, the home must be made suicide-proof. This can never be completely accomplished; however, I ask parents to remove all firearms, dispose of all unused medicines, lock up the keys to the cars, and remove all ropes or cords that could be used for hanging. Making the method for self-destruction less accessible gives the teen more time to consider options other than suicide.

| "While access to firearms ... and particular mental disorders may be determining factors in whether someone attempts suicide, they are not the sole reasons."

MANY FACTORS CONTRIBUTE TO TEEN SUICIDE

Andrea Young Ward

Depression and access to firearms are frequently blamed for teen suicides, but Andrea Young Ward maintains in the following viewpoint that many other factors are often involved. She argues that feelings of hopelessness and alienation, homosexuality, concerns about AIDS, and other problems can be overwhelming for teens, who may feel that suicide will stop their pain. Ward also contends that the increasing availability of drugs and alcohol may play a role in the rise in teenage suicide rates. Ward is a freelance writer in Berkeley, California. The names of the suicide survivors in the following viewpoint have been changed to protect their privacy.

As you read, consider the following questions:

1. What rank does suicide hold as a cause of death among teenagers, according to the Centers for Disease Control and Prevention, as cited by Ward?
2. What feeling is more predictive of suicide than depression, in Alan Berman's opinion, as quoted by the author?
3. In Miller Newton's opinion, as cited by Ward, what percentage of teen suicides are drug- and alcohol-related?

Abridged from Andrea Young Ward, "The Question of Life," *Common Boundary*, July/August 1996. Copyright 1996 by Andrea Young Ward. Reprinted with permission of the author.

As a young woman, Maria could envision no promising future. Although she was a talented painter and costume designer, she found that she was at the end of a five-year life plan and nowhere near her goals. Antidepressant medication proved powerless over her nearly debilitating depression, later diagnosed as bipolar affective disorder. With little hope of earning a living in the creative arts and seeing few other possibilities, she finally decided on her 24th birthday that she would commit suicide.

Now 40, Maria is articulate and upbeat, but she often speaks of her attempt in the present tense, as though somewhere inside her the younger Maria is reliving it over and over. As the child of an alcoholic household, Maria says, she knew no coping skills to deal with her situation. "I could go into suicidal feelings instantly—any kind of disappointment or rejection triggered it," she recalls. "Everything that is normally very vibrant and colorful turns into a black-and-white TV set."

Despite having set her sights on self-destruction, Maria was careful not to inconvenience anyone else with her plans. She decided that her date of death would be July 4, when her roommate would be out of town. Because she put on a convincing facade to her friends and even her psychiatrist, none of them suspected that her apparent sense of relief was a result of her decision to die. She began giving away her possessions, while storing antidepressant prescriptions. Says Maria: "I began the descent into believing that the best option I had in my life was to die."

A TIMELESS PHENOMENON

Suicide is a timeless phenomenon, but it is becoming pandemic in our time. People are killing themselves more often and at younger ages. From 1952 through 1992, the incidence of suicide among adolescents and young adults (those younger than 25) nearly tripled, making suicide the third leading cause of death for that age group, according to the Centers for Disease Control and Prevention (CDC). A 1994 Gallup Organization survey found that 12 percent of young people between the ages of 13 and 19 had come close to committing suicide, while 5 percent had actually attempted suicide; another 59 percent said they personally knew a teenager who had attempted it.

While access to firearms, the most common method for carrying out suicides, and particular mental disorders may be determining factors in whether someone attempts suicide, they are not the sole reasons. Factors such as AIDS, homosexuality, and access to drugs can complicate the already bewildering time of adolescence and young adulthood, turning the transition to independence into an emotional minefield that for many people is simply too overwhelming to negotiate.

HOPELESSNESS, NOT DEPRESSION

"Vincent van Gogh once said that sadness lasts a lifetime," wrote Paul Eppinger in his last letter to his father. "I would add that the sorrow grows deeper every day, for those of us who have been cursed with the sensitivity to comprehend what is, and the imagination to perceive how it should have been." After three previous attempts beginning when he was 16, Paul killed himself at age 29.

Although many assume that people like Paul are depressed, it is not always the case. According to many experts, feelings of hopelessness—that "there are no solutions to my problem"—are more predictive of suicidal risk than diagnoses of depression per se. "I tend to believe that being depressed itself is not a sufficient cause to lead to or explain suicide," says Alan L. Berman, Ph.D., executive director of the American Association of Suicidology. "Hopelessness is a much more abject way of thinking and feeling."

THREE SIGNIFICANT FACTORS

There are three significant factors in teenage suicide, says pediatrician Diane Sacks. "The first is depression. Why don't we treat kids who are depressed? Because we are ashamed of mental illness. The second thing is firearms—"it's not a question of keeping them under lock and key but of keeping them out of the house." The third factor: alcohol. "Many suicides," says Sacks, "are done after kids have been drinking." In fact, says Sacks, "a significant number" of teenage deaths in car accidents are really suicides where alcohol was a factor.

Rae Corelli, *Maclean's*, January 29, 1996.

Miller Newton, M.Div., Ph.D., president and clinical director of KIDS of New Jersey, an adolescent treatment program, and author of *Adolescence: Guiding Youth Through the Perilous Ordeal*, says that, particularly in teenagers, a "trapped" feeling or a feeling of desperation is a more accurate precursor to suicide than depression. "Both depression and desperation are states of unhappiness—but depression is more slowed down," he says.

Charles Eppinger, Paul's father and, according to Paul, his "best friend," says he does not believe that his son was depressed, although feelings of helplessness often overtook him.

Charles—who has collected Paul's journals and letters in the book *Restless Mind, Quiet Thoughts: A Personal Journal*—points out that Paul used the word "depressed" only once in referring to himself and that he was very careful with words. "While I am not a psychotherapist, I wonder if depression is not too much of a generic term that doesn't often help us in dealing with people who have more severe problems."

Although Charles is quick to say that he is not trying to indict society for his son's death, his words suggest that it is important to look not just at the problems within an individual but also at the relationship between the suicidal person and the world in which he or she lives. Charles points out that Paul was resourceful and hard-working, but that he continually struggled with finding a balance between "making a living" and maintaining a sense of creativity, spontaneity, and genuineness. Paul wrote poetry and short stories, sculpted, and did fine woodworking; he was interested in architecture and was working as a carpenter when he died. He often sought the solace of nature, retreating to the woods for days at a time in order to search for meaning and tranquillity. "It wasn't that he was lazy or lacked discipline or wasn't willing to make a contribution," says Charles. "He worked hard, he was resourceful, he tried time after time. He knew he was unusual, but he couldn't figure out why that didn't count."

A FIXATION ON PAIN

Maria, the artist who attempted suicide at age 24, remembers being in a state of "tunnel vision" for four months between the time she decided to kill herself and her actual attempt. According to Richard Heckler, psychologist and author of *Waking Up, Alive: The Descent, the Suicide Attempt, and the Return to Life*, all people who attempt suicide experience such a trance, which he defines as a narrowing of perception in which one fixates on one's pain and can imagine no other future. "If you can't imagine the future being any different, then suicide seems a logical option to stop the pain," he says.

Maria describes the methodical plan for her death the way some might describe picking a picnic spot. "I'd scoped out a place where I wanted to die: a beautiful meadow. I laid out the sleeping bag, put limbs over it so it would be hidden. I got in the bag, took all the pills. This is what I wanted out of life: to die this way. I'd go to sleep looking at the moon."

Maria had fasted the week before to be sure her body would absorb the pills, then had eaten a light meal to get her stomach used to eating again. She was sure she would be dead within three hours. But like many other survivors of attempts, she underestimated her body's ability to hold on to life. Almost a day later, a passerby looking for a lost animal stumbled across Maria, who lay in a coma, her breathing slowed to once every five minutes. She was declared dead when she reached the hospital, but a team of residents resuscitated her heart. Maria's body, independent of her will, struggled back to life.

Not surprisingly, at first she wasn't happy to be alive. "This is like screwing with my personal power," she recalls of failing to kill herself. "Now I'm in this no man's land of having my life back. But what do I do with it?" With time, she decided to serve people, feeling that she had to pay the world back for her life. She went to dental school and now works as a dental assistant. "Serving others became the way I plugged back into life," she says.

Stephen Levine, author of *Who Dies?* and other books on death and dying, calls service the key to transforming suicidal thinking. As he puts it, one can respond either, "Life sucks—I'll kill myself," or "Life sucks—I'd better get to work." He says that suicidal people tend to think they are not valid human beings, but serving others in a homeless shelter or in a soup kitchen, for example, can remind them of their own worth, and hence restore their will to live.

SOMETIMES LIFE IS PAINFUL

Tanya did not feel at home in her midwestern, fundamentalist family when she twice attempted to take her life, at age 14 and again at age 16. Now 23, she has a candid and direct manner, laughs easily, and drives a shiny sports car with a "No Fear" sticker plastered across her windshield. Save for the thick scars on her forearms, which she reveals from under the sleeves of her white sweatshirt, she looks like a typical college-aged woman.

"I would have liked for someone to talk to me not about not doing it, but about why I wanted to do it—to acknowledge that the feelings were there and try to figure out why they were there," says Tanya. "I wanted people to say, 'Why do you feel this bad?' No one ever asked me that."

Levine says that many counselors add to a teenager's feelings of isolation by denying them. "When you are working with suicidal teenagers," he says, "you have to come from your own broken heart." In his view, a counselor should be able to sit down with a teenager and say: "Yes, life just *sucks* sometimes. It is so painful. I am amazed more people don't kill themselves. It's okay that you feel that way. It's *not* okay that you kill yourself."

Some of the reasons Tanya felt bad were that her father, with whom she had only recently come into contact, died unexpectedly right before her first attempt, a schoolmate had committed suicide two months before, and Tanya was also wrestling with an emerging awareness of her homosexuality. She says that, although she did not yet consider herself a lesbian, she felt confused and isolated within her fundamentalist Christian family and church, where she says "anyone who is gay is like the enemy."

Tanya's story highlights a controversial aspect of teen suicide—the link between it and sexual orientation. The first large-scale, government-sponsored study on the subject is still being conducted [as of 1996] by officials from the CDC and the National Institute of Mental Health. A 1989 report by the Department of Health and Human Services, based on interviews with 500 gay and lesbian youths in San Francisco, found that 30 percent of those interviewed had attempted suicide at least once. However, other research revealed conflicting results. A 1993 study conducted by the Columbia University College of Physicians and Surgeons, for example, found that of 120 youth suicides in New York City, only 2.5 percent were gay or lesbian.

Suicide in general is believed by Newton and other experts to be underreported because of family members' shame and because many incidents are misunderstood as accidents. In the case of gay teens, survivors and family members often experience additional shame surrounding the homosexuality itself, thus hampering the gathering of reliable statistics linking it with suicide. There simply are no hard facts on the matter, and some claim that not enough studies have been conducted because of the issue's political nature.

A SENSE OF ALIENATION

Regardless of its source, the sense of being an outsider is shared by many suicidal people. Experts say that feelings of alienation can be intensified by other forms of prejudice such as racism, but even teenagers who come from white, middle-class families often experience them. According to Heckler, the delicate balance all adolescents must deal with is feeling connected to a human lineage while finding and expressing their individuality. Ours is a particularly rigid culture, he says, in which certain forms of individuality are seen negatively. In a society that does not always welcome the different colors, shapes, and expressions adolescence takes, the balance between becoming an individual and feeling connected with others can become strained.

"There are some people who consistently end up feeling isolated and alienated and are progressively pushed to the periphery of the culture," says Heckler. "It's hard to commit suicide when you feel connection."

Heckler adds that ours is mostly a "death-phobic" culture and suicide a virtual taboo. The number of suicides could be halved if people in this country would simply talk about it, he believes. "People who contemplate suicide and people who have attempted suicide, for the most part, keep their stories secret for fear that they will be seen as crazy or contagious, or that they might make someone else feel uncomfortable," says Heckler. We must create a culture, he says, in which it is acceptable to discuss suicide and feelings of hopelessness. For example, these ideas could be addressed in the educational system, he adds.

Finding that one in five of its 1994 survey respondents said he or she would not know where to turn for help if having suicidal thoughts, the Gallup Organization came to a conclusion similar to Heckler's. "Careful consideration should be given to support groups," its report states, "in which young people can open up their lives to friends in a confidential setting. Such groups can be particularly powerful if there is a spiritual dimension."

Even Paul Eppinger, who ultimately did not survive the tortured isolation of his youth, had an inkling of what might have saved him. "All I know," he wrote, "is that the few times I have truly touched and have been touched by another person—those few times when I have really seen, and likewise been acknowledged as a reality and not a projection—the reward, the pure exhilarating freshness, was unmistakable."

A WAY TO STOP THE PAIN

As a young person, Richard always felt like an outsider. The son of Mexican immigrants, he says, "I didn't fit in an Anglo world." At age 11 he tried to hang himself from a tree. At 13 he held a revolver in his mouth until a friend found and stopped him. Later, he tried to overdose on heroin four times and on several other occasions swallowed poison and pills. Each time, he was found and somehow saved. "Suicide was a way of life for me," he says.

After his first attempt, Richard became a gang member and was using heroin by age 14. For much of his life he battled drug addiction, and he spent 12 and a half years in and out of prison. "Even though people saw me as a happy guy, I was always very sad and lonely and in despair," he says. "As much as I loved life, I didn't like the world. You see, it's not that you want to end your life; you want a change from the situation going on right now."

According to Levine, Richard's sentiment is shared by most other suicidal people. "People don't kill themselves because they hate life as much as they kill themselves because the love they have for life is not requited," he says.

Heckler agrees that suicidal people do not really want to die. "If there was a way for them to stop the pain and not die, they would choose that," he says.

THE ROLE OF DRUGS

While it may be tempting to blame young people's despair on today's societal conditions, Richard's youth in the 1950s illustrates that many problems such as gangs and drug abuse are not unique to the '90s. Newton believes that adolescent suicide has risen dramatically in the past few decades because drugs have become more accessible to teens. He says that 85 percent of all adolescent suicides are drug- and alcohol-related but that this fact is often overlooked because the suicide frequently occurs after the full effect of the drug, usually alcohol, has worn off. He says that most suicidal teens have a healthy sense of self-esteem and come from "normal" families. They begin using drugs as a result of peer pressure but end up upsetting the chemical balance of their brains, impairing both mood and judgment.

Newton's theory brings up a chicken-and-egg dilemma: Do kids use drugs and thus become suicidal? Or do they start using drugs because they experience despair and isolation? Newton says the former; others claim the latter. For his part, Richard says he used drugs "to escape the pain of life." Suicidal people, he says, "get hurt easily by the changing moods of the world."

AIDS

Certainly, there are a lot of changing moods to be felt today. Aside from the myriad technological and sociological changes that have taken place since the 1950s, when suicide rates began to soar, the reality of AIDS has become unavoidable for young people today. According to the CDC, as of the end of 1994, 14,104 American males and 4,436 American females between the ages of 13 and 24 years were infected with HIV. A study conducted by Cornell University Medical Center in 1989 found that people with AIDS were 36 times more likely to attempt suicide than those without AIDS at a comparable age. While suicide among the chronically or terminally ill is in many ways a separate topic from those who kill themselves mainly out of mental anguish, it is hard to ignore the psychological impact of the AIDS threat on the first generation to have it as part of growing up.

Heckler says that young people's connection to the future is severed by the disease, as it was a generation ago by the threat of the atomic bomb. "In some ways, AIDS is this generation's equivalent of nuclear holocaust, except that it really has exploded, so it's even worse," he says, explaining that AIDS creates a more pervasive sense of anomie and hopelessness.

At the heart of suicide, Heckler believes, are the seeds of transformation. "People who are suicidal have the right idea," he says. "There is something inside them that does need to die—some set of relationships, some way of seeing the world. Something that is not working for them does need to die, but it's not them."

PERIODICAL BIBLIOGRAPHY

The following articles have been selected to supplement the diverse views presented in this chapter. Addresses are provided for periodicals not indexed in the *Readers' Guide to Periodical Literature*, the *Alternative Press Index*, the *Social Sciences Index*, or the *Index to Legal Periodicals and Books*.

John Colapinto	"Getting Lost: Chronicle of a Death Foretold," *Rolling Stone*, October 17, 1996.
Rae Corelli	"Killing the Pain," *Maclean's*, January 29, 1996.
Douglas Foster	"The Disease Is Adolescence," *Rolling Stone*, December 9, 1993.
Donna Gaines	"Suicidal Tendencies: Kurt Did Not Die for You," *Rolling Stone*, June 2, 1994.
David Gelman	"The Mystery of Suicide," *Newsweek*, April 18, 1994.
Elizabeth Karlsberg	"'I Wanted to Die': Teens and Suicide," *Teen*, August 1993.
Scott McLemee	"Sell the Kids for Food," *In These Times*, May 2, 1994.
David Shaffer	"Political Science," *New Yorker*, May 3, 1993.
Fern Shen	"Where Suicide Rates Are Soaring," *Washington Post National Weekly Edition*, July 29–August 4, 1996. Available from Reprints, 1150 15th St. NW, Washington, DC 20071.
Steven Stack and Jim Gundlach	"The Effect of Country Music on Suicide," *Social Forces*, September 1992. Available from 110 Manning Hall, University of North Carolina, Chapel Hill, NC 27599-3355.
Steven Stack, Jim Gundlach, and Jimmie L. Reeves	"The Heavy Metal Subculture and Suicide," *Suicide and Life-Threatening Behavior*, vol. 24, no. 1, Spring 1994. Available from The Guilford Press, 72 Spring St., New York, NY 10012.
Teen	"The Heartbreaking Reality of Suicide Pacts," August 1996.
Teen	"I Tried to Commit Suicide Because My Boyfriend Broke Up with Me," October 1995.
Wataru Tsurumi	"A Final Exit for Japan's Generation X," *Harper's Magazine*, January 1994.
Harry F. Waters et al.	"Teenage Suicide: One Act Not to Follow," *Newsweek*, April 18, 1994.

SHOULD ASSISTED SUICIDE BE LEGAL?

CHAPTER PREFACE

Before Dr. Jack Kevorkian focused national attention on the issue of assisted suicide by helping a patient commit suicide in 1990, terminally ill patients were dying with the quiet aid of families and doctors in homes and hospitals across the United States. With his suicide machine, Kevorkian changed assisted suicide from a little-discussed practice into a national issue argued in front of the U.S. Supreme Court.

Critics of assisted suicide often use the terms *assisted suicide* and *euthanasia* interchangeably, but important differences exist between the two practices. During an assisted suicide, the potential suicide victim, generally a terminally ill patient, specifically asks someone—usually a physician, family member, or friend—for help in dying. The helper may provide lethal medication or some other means of dying, but the patient alone is responsible for the final act.

During euthanasia, on the other hand, someone other than the patient is directly responsible for causing the patient's death. Passive euthanasia occurs when vital medical treatment—such as medication, a respirator, or a feeding tube—is discontinued and the patient allowed to die from the natural consequences of the terminal illness or injury. In active euthanasia, a physician, family member, or friend directly causes the patient's death—for example, by giving the patient a lethal injection. The patient dies from the injection, not from the effects of the terminal disease or injury. Both passive and active euthanasia can be voluntary or involuntary; in other words, either type of euthanasia may be performed with the knowledge and consent of the patient (voluntary) or without such knowledge and consent (involuntary).

Opponents of assisted suicide argue that legalizing the procedure will lead down a slippery slope toward the acceptance and/or legalization of voluntary euthanasia and, ultimately, to the practice of involuntary euthanasia. Supporters of assisted suicide contend that giving physicians the right to help their patients die will not lead to involuntary euthanasia and that the best way to prevent abuse of assisted suicide is to regulate the practice. The moral, ethical, and legal aspects of assisted suicide are debated by the authors in the following chapter.

> "We are already engaged in physician-assisted suicide—we just aren't calling it that."

PHYSICIAN-ASSISTED SUICIDE SHOULD BE LEGALIZED

Robert T. Hall

In the following viewpoint, Robert T. Hall contends that withdrawing life-sustaining treatments from dying patients is a common, legal, and painful method of physician-assisted suicide. However, Hall asserts, many terminally ill patients who wish to end their suffering are not undergoing life-sustaining treatment and therefore would require more assistance from their doctor, such as a drug overdose. In such cases, physician-assisted suicide is an ethical and humane course, he argues, and the practice should be legalized. Hall is a professor of sociology and philosophy at West Virginia State College in Institute and the author of several books and articles on morality and ethics.

As you read, consider the following questions:

1. What are two common criticisms of physician-assisted suicide, according to Hall?
2. In the author's opinion, what policies would ensure that physician-assisted suicide is employed only when no other treatment options are beneficial?
3. Why would legalizing physician-assisted suicide increase the public's trust of and respect for the medical profession, in Hall's view?

From Robert T. Hall, "Final Act: Sorting Out the Ethics of Physician-Assisted Suicide," *Humanist*, November/December 1994. Reprinted by permission of the author.

The question of whether a physician should assist a patient with an intolerable terminal condition to end his or her life has been debated since the practice of medicine began. Philosophically, it's been a toss-up: Plato, Thomas More, Francis Bacon, David Hume, and Jeremy Bentham approved; Aristotle, Thomas Aquinas, Roger Bacon, John Locke, and Karl Marx did not.

In the United States, patients now generally have a legal right to refuse treatment, and physicians can honor advance directives and surrogate decisions. So physicians currently withhold or withdraw treatment—respiratory support, CPR, dialysis, sometimes nutrition and hydration—thereby allowing patients to die. Studies indicate that, as of 1991, roughly half of the deaths in hospital settings in nonemergency cases involved some form of withholding or withdrawing of treatment. A 1989 study reported that 85 to 90 percent of critical-care physicians are withholding or withdrawing life-saving or life-sustaining treatment from some patients. . . .

PHYSICIAN-ASSISTED SUICIDE

The type of case most directly associated with physician-assisted suicide in current discussion is one in which a conscious and competent patient asks the physician to take some action that will bring about his or her death or to provide the means for the patient or the patient's family to take the action. Cases that fall into this category often involve the gradual disintegration of the powers and capacities which make us human: severe instances of amyotrophic lateral sclerosis, multiple sclerosis, Parkinson's disease, Lupus, end-stage lung disease, and perhaps advanced brain cancer or gastric cancer. There are patients in some of these conditions, although probably not very many, for whom hospice care does not work effectively. They suffer not so much pain as the deterioration of their bodily functions and mental capacities, and the misery of deterioration can be a long and costly process. The most compelling argument in favor of physician-assisted suicide has always been the one based upon the fact that some conditions are so intolerable that the only relief is death, and the patient wishes to end the suffering rather than to have it prolonged. Sensitive and courageous human beings have often responded to these situations in the past by assisting the sufferer to put an end to his or her misery. They are now doing this more openly and more often. The question is whether this will be done with the assistance and regulation of the medical profession or whether it will remain covert.

The most recent answer to such problems, which may well

become standard practice, is to sedate these patients into complete unconsciousness and to withhold nutrition and hydration until they die. This relieves the patient of any conscious experience of his or her condition. It also shows just how far we will go to preserve the myth that only "passive" euthanasia is morally acceptable. We should face the facts: complete sedation and the withdrawal of food and water is active euthanasia, and it is probably not the best method. [Passive euthanasia is commonly defined as allowing a terminally ill patient to die by witholding life-sustaining treatment. Active euthanasia occurs when someone actively and directly takes the life of a terminally ill or dying patient.] Some patients in extreme conditions might choose this method, but the clear choice of others, if they could have their way, would be to end it all sooner than such a method allows and spare themselves and their families the agony.

Our society, of course, legally forces us into this sham since the patient only has the legal right to refuse treatment. Unfortunately, some of the patients in these extreme conditions are not lucky enough to have a life-saving treatment that can be stopped. If death is their only relief, they need help. The proper response, ethically, is to change the standards of practice and the law, if necessary, to permit the physician to assist either directly or indirectly. Proposals to decriminalize physician assistance, such as the 1994 Oregon Right to Die initiative [under a restraining order until a federal appeals court overturned the injunction in February 1997], generally take into account the ethical imperatives of relieving suffering and respecting patient choice. The law should ensure, through a second medical opinion if necessary, that assistance will only be available if and when a competent physician judges that there is no other way left to relieve the patient of his or her misery.

QUESTIONS AND ANSWERS

The problem of physician-assisted suicide poses a double question and requires a double answer. Critics often charge that, if physician-assisted suicide were legalized, patients who are mentally unstable or simply depressed would too quickly choose suicide. But current laws stipulate clearly that no physician should ever offer or agree to any medical procedure unless he or she is convinced that it is in the best interests of the patient. With regard to physician-assisted suicide, the physician would have to be convinced that nothing else could be done and that the situation was so intolerable to the patient that an easier death was in his or her best interests.

The other popular criticism is the reverse: if physicians alone decide when there is no hope left for a meaningful life, we will be on the slippery slope toward the killing of people with any and every sort of disability. The answer here is that current laws already require informed consent for any medical treatment: physician-assisted suicide would have to remain strictly at the patient's informed request. People should, of course, be allowed to express their wishes through living wills and surrogate decision-makers as long as these means are used to enact the patient's wishes. (The problem with the Nancy Cruzan case, in which the family of a woman in a permanent vegetative state attempted to have her life support removed, was not that the law required evidence of the patient's wishes but that the legal standard of proof was too high.)

THE SACREDNESS OF LIFE

I, for one, am no longer willing to be silent on this issue. I, as a Christian, want to state publicly my present conclusions. After much internal wrestling, I can now say with conviction that I favor both active and passive euthanasia, and I also believe that assisted suicide should be legalized, but only under circumstances that would effectively preclude both self-interest and malevolence. . . .

My conclusions are based on the conviction that the sacredness of my life is not ultimately found in my biological extension. It is found rather in the touch, the smile and the love of those to whom I can knowingly respond. When that ability to respond disappears permanently, so, I believe, does the meaning and the value of my biological life. Even my hope of life beyond biological death is vested in a living relationship with the God who, my faith tradition teaches me, calls me by name. I believe that the image of God is formed in me by my ability to respond to that calling Deity. If that is so, then the image of God has moved beyond my mortal body when my ability to respond consciously to that Divine Presence disappears. So nothing sacred is compromised by assisting my death in those circumstances.

John Shelby Spong, *Human Quest*, May/June 1996.

The critics of physician-assisted suicide thus attempt to make a case against euthanasia by pointing out that, if physicians *alone* decide when life is worth saving, they would engage in involuntary euthanasia; but on the other hand, if patients *alone* can choose when to end their lives, suicide would be permitted for emotional or psychological reasons. The answer to this criticism is that the choice should never be up to physicians or patients *alone*; it should require mutual agreement. And this is exactly what the most widely held principles of medical ethics require. The principle of beneficence requires that physicians do only what is in the patient's interest, and the principle of autonomy requires that treatment be administered only at the patient's request. Taken together, as they must be, a morally justifiable decision could only be made when the physician and patient came to an agreement. Neither the physician alone nor the patient alone could or should decide. The critics' case can only be made by considering each half of the moral imperative in isolation.

Furthermore, in most states these ethical principles are already embodied in statutory or case law regarding informed consent. Informed consent requires that the procedure is adequately explained and understood by the patient; that the alternatives and their possible consequences are explained as well; and that the patient is able to make an informed decision in the light of his or her own values.

SOCIETY IS READY

By many indications, American society is quite ready for the legalization of physician assistance at death. A 1991 General Social Survey conducted by the National Opinion Research Center asked the question:

> When a person has a disease that cannot be cured, do you think doctors should be allowed by law to end the patient's life by some painless means if the patient and his or her family request it?

Of the 1,024 people in the national random sample who responded, 70 percent said "yes," 25 percent said "no," and 5 percent didn't know. A November 1993 Harris poll, which explained the safeguards proposed in the Oregon Right to Die initiative, found 73 percent approval.

At present, there is more reason to be concerned about current medical practice in treating terminally ill patients than about the legalization of physician-assisted suicide. The more we shy away from recognizing the true nature of the current practices of withholding and withdrawing treatment, . . . the more likely we are to find ourselves on the slippery slope toward involuntary euthanasia.

Some physicians now take the position that they would be willing to provide the means for a patient to take his or her own life but would not want to assist the patient directly. Aside from cases in which this is physically impossible—for example, if the patient cannot take pills—the physician should want to ensure that the medication provided will actually be taken by the patient and not by a distraught spouse.

TRUST AND RESPECT

Another common concern among physicians is that legalizing physician-assisted suicide will diminish the trust that patients have in their physicians. This is based upon the simplistic assumption that trust implies only that physicians will do no harm. The fact is that many patients now want to trust that their physicians will stay with them and will not abandon them when the only way out of their suffering is to help them to die as they choose. The medical profession as a whole will gain public respect if it agrees to medicalize the dying process rather than leaving the final act to be performed with handguns, plastic bags, and illegally acquired drugs.

If we face up to the realities of current practice, we should admit that we are already engaged in physician-assisted suicide—we just aren't calling it that. Decriminalizing physician assistance under the current guidelines of beneficent standards of practice and informed-consent laws would expand the options available and would put physicians in a better position to help those who now have no other way out. It would surely be better to have the practice regulated than to allow the further development of self-help methods.

| "Physician-assisted suicide, once legal, will not stay confined to the terminally ill and mentally competent."

PHYSICIAN-ASSISTED SUICIDE SHOULD NOT BE LEGALIZED

Leon R. Kass

Leon R. Kass argues in the following viewpoint that legalizing physician-assisted suicide will have extremely dangerous consequences for individuals and society. The legalization of physician-assisted suicide will irrevocably damage the doctor-patient relationship, Kass maintains, as doctors will be transformed from healers into prescribers of death. He asserts that if physician-assisted suicide becomes legal, the elderly, terminally ill, and disabled will feel it is their duty to choose suicide. Furthermore, Kass contends, legalizing physician-assisted suicide will lead to the acceptance of euthanasia performed without the patient's consent. Kass is an ethicist, physician, and biochemist at the University of Chicago.

As you read, consider the following questions:

1. According to Kass, what is the inviolable rule of the Hippocratic Oath?
2. Why is the practice of physician-assisted suicide unregulable, in the author's opinion?
3. What is the difference between physician-assisted suicide and the cessation of treatment, according to Kass?

From Leon R. Kass, "Dehumanization Triumphant, " First Things, August/September 1996. Reprinted by permission of First Things, a publication of the Institute on Religion & Public Life, New York, N.Y.

Efforts to legalize physician-assisted suicide and to establish a constitutional "right to die" are deeply troubling events, morally dubious in themselves, extremely dangerous in their likely consequences. The legalization of physician-assisted suicide, ostensibly a measure enhancing the freedom of dying patients, is in fact a deadly license for physicians to prescribe death, free from outside scrutiny and immune from possible prosecution. The manufacture of a "right to die," ostensibly a gift to those not dying fast enough, is, in fact, the state's abdication of its duty to protect innocent life and its abandonment especially of the old, the weak, and the poor.

FROM HEALER TO DISPENSER OF DEATH

The legalization of physician-assisted suicide will pervert the medical profession by transforming the healer of human beings into a technical dispenser of death. For over two millennia the medical ethic, mindful that power to cure is also power to kill, has held as an inviolable rule, "Doctors must not kill." The venerable Hippocratic Oath clearly rules out physician-assisted suicide. Without this taboo, medicine ceases to be a trustworthy and ethical profession; without it, all of us will suffer—yes, more than we suffer now because some of us die too slowly.

The doctor-patient relationship will be damaged. The patient's trust in the doctor's devotion to the patient's best interests will be hard to sustain once doctors can legally prescribe death. Even conscientious physicians will have trouble caring wholeheartedly for patients once death becomes a "therapeutic option." The prohibition against killing patients, medicine's first principle of ethical self-restraint, recognizes that no physician devoted to the benefit of the sick can serve the patient by making him dead. The physician-suicide-assistant or physician-euthanizer is a deadly self-contradiction.

Physician-assisted suicide, once legal, will not stay confined to the terminally ill and mentally competent who freely and knowingly elect it for themselves. Requests will be engineered and choices manipulated by those who control the information, and, manipulation aside, many elderly and incurable people will experience a right to choose death *as their duty* to do so. Moreover, the vast majority of those who are said to "merit" "a humane and dignified death" do not fall in this category and cannot request it for themselves. Persons with mental illness or Alzheimer's disease, deformed infants, and retarded or dying children would thus be denied our new humane "aid-in-dying." But not to worry. The lawyers, encouraged by the cost-containers, will sue to rectify this inequity. Why, they will argue, should the comatose or the demented be denied a right to assisted suicide just because they cannot claim it for themselves? With court-appointed proxy consentors, we will quickly erase the distinction between the right to choose one's own death and the right to request someone else's.

AN UNREGULABLE PRACTICE

The termination of lives someone else thinks are no longer worth living is now occurring on a large scale in Holland, where assisted suicide and euthanasia have been practiced by physicians for more than a decade, under "safeguards" more stringent than those enacted in the 1994 Oregon law [legalizing physician-assisted suicide]. According to the Dutch government's own alarming figures, there are over one thousand cases per year of direct involuntary euthanasia; also 8,100 cases of morphine overdosage intending to terminate life, 61 percent without the patient's consent. Although the guidelines insist that choosing death must be informed and voluntary, over 40 percent of Dutch physicians have performed involuntary euthanasia. As the Dutch have shown, the practice of assisted suicide is in principle unregulable, because it is cloaked in the privacy of the doctor-patient relationship.

ABUSE AND EXPLOITATION

If those advocating legalization of assisted suicide prevail, it will be a reflection that as a culture we are turning away from efforts to improve our care of the mentally ill, the infirm, and the elderly. Instead, we would be licensing the right to abuse and exploit the fears of the ill and depressed. We would be accepting the view of those who are depressed and suicidal that death is the preferred solution to the problems of illness, age, and depression.

Herbert Hendin and Gerald Klerman, *American Journal of Psychiatry*, January 1993.

Legalizing assisted suicide would mark a drastic change in the social and political order. The state would be surrendering its monopoly on the legal use of lethal force, a monopoly it holds under the social contract, a monopoly it needs if it is to protect innocent life, its first responsibility. It should surprise no one if physicians, once they are exempted from the ban on the private use of lethal force, wind up killing without restraint. Here, by the way, is a *genuine* violation of the Fourteenth Amendment: deprivation of life without due process of law.

We must care for the dying, not make them dead. By accepting mortality yet knowing that we will not kill, doctors can focus on enhancing the lives of those who are dying, with relief of pain and discomfort, moral and social support, and, when appropriate, the removal of technical interventions that are merely useless or degrading additions to the burdens of dying—including, frequently, hospitalization itself. Doctors must not intentionally kill, or help to kill, but they may allow a patient to die.

Ceasing medical intervention, allowing nature to take its course, differs fundamentally from assisting suicide and active euthanasia. Not the physician, but the underlying fatal illness becomes the true cause of death. More important morally, in ceasing treatment the physician *does not intend the death* of the patient, even if death follows as a result. Rather, he seeks to avoid useless and degrading medical additions to the already sad end of a life. In contrast, in assisted suicide the physician necessarily intends primarily that the patient be made dead.

AN IMPORTANT DISTINCTION

One cannot exaggerate the importance of the distinction between withholding or withdrawing treatment and directly killing, a distinction foolishly dismissed in the Second and Ninth Court of Appeals' decisions [concerning assisted suicide in Washington and New York]. Both as a matter of law and as a matter of medical ethics, the right to refuse unwanted medical intervention is properly seen not as part of a right to become dead but rather as part of a *right protecting how we choose to live*, even while we are dying.

Once we refuse the technical fix, physicians and the rest of us can also rise to the occasion: we can learn to act humanly in the presence of finitude. Far more than adequate morphine and the removal of burdensome chemotherapy, the dying need our presence and our encouragement. Withdrawal of human contact, affection, and care is the greatest single cause of the dehumanization of dying. People who care for autonomy and dignity should try to correct this dehumanization of the end of life, instead of giving dehumanization its final triumph by welcoming the desperate good-bye-to-all-that contained in one final plea for poison. Not the alleged humaneness of an elixir of death, but the humanness of connected living-while-dying is what medicine—and the rest of us—most owe the dying. The treatment of choice is and always will be company and care.

"When the assistant is motivated by compassion for an incurably ill patient who clearly and repeatedly requests help, [assisted suicide] can be ethical and moral."

PHYSICIAN–ASSISTED SUICIDE IS MORAL

Timothy E. Quill

Timothy E. Quill is a doctor who helped a terminally ill patient, "Diane," commit suicide and then wrote about the experience in 1991 in the *New England Journal of Medicine*. He is also one of the plaintiffs who successfully challenged New York's law against assisted suicide in the Ninth Circuit Court of Appeals (as of April 1997 this case was under consideration by the U.S. Supreme Court). The following viewpoint is an excerpt from Quill's book *Death and Dignity: Making Choices and Taking Charge*, in which Quill argues that doctors who help their terminally ill patients to commit suicide out of compassion for their suffering are acting ethically and morally, while those who purposely undermedicate such patients to prevent potential suicides by overdosing are unethical and immoral.

As you read, consider the following questions:

1. According to Quill, when should a suicide attempt be prevented?
2. What is the difference between physician-assisted suicide and voluntary euthanasia, according to the author?
3. What is the distinction between passive euthanasia and active euthanasia, in Quill's view?

The debate about physician-assisted death thus far has been clouded by imprecise, sometimes inflammatory use of language. The descriptive term "physician-assisted death" includes both physician-assisted suicide and voluntary active euthanasia. It emphasizes the physician's role as an assistant to an act initiated by the patient. Doctors "killing" patients is technically correct, but it incorrectly suggests a physician-driven act, and brings out uneasy visions of the Holocaust, in which a vicious abuse of physician power was used to systematically exterminate those who were deemed to be socially unworthy. Nothing could be further from the intent of those who favor a limited reconsideration of public policy in the areas of assisted suicide and voluntary active euthanasia. Physicians are reluctant partners in assisted dying, motivated by the compassion they feel toward suffering patients who request their help and have no good alternatives.

THE DIFFERENT KINDS OF SUICIDE

Suicide is defined as the intentional taking of one's own life, but its multilayered meaning emerges in a second definition which includes the self-destruction of one's own personal interests. In the medical literature, suicide is almost always viewed as an act of despair and self-destructiveness, the outgrowth of untreated depression and impaired rational thought. Suicide in that context is clearly something to be prevented, and physicians' appropriate role is to use all their resources, including enforced hospitalization if necessary, to help patients regain their will to live.

Suicide in the context of end-stage medical illness associated with irreversible suffering that can only end in death can have a different meaning. Many believe that suicide under such circumstances can be rational—it is hard to judge the wish for an end to intolerable suffering that can only end in death as irrational. Under such tragic circumstances, death can sometimes provide the only relief. The only question is, how much more one must endure until it comes. Yet, because patients with such severe medical conditions are usually sad if not clinically depressed, it can at times be difficult to determine whether emotional responses to their illnesses are distorting their decision making. If there is any question that depression or other mental illness is coloring the patient's judgment, then consultation by an experienced psychiatrist or psychologist is necessary to understand the full implications of an incurably ill patient's request for assisted death.

In "assisted suicide," a patient is still carrying out his own act, but he is indirectly helped by an "assistant." When the assistant is motivated by compassion for an incurably ill patient who clearly and repeatedly requests help, the act can be ethical and moral, if not legal. If the assistant is motivated by greed, or if there is uncertainty about the rationality or motivation behind the patient's request, then the act of assistance becomes immoral, unethical, as well as illegal. There is little case-based legal definition for what kind of compassionate "assistance" might be considered illegal. For example, a physician might prescribe a potentially lethal supply of medication, along with information about what dose would be lethal and what dose would be medicinal. There the physician's intention could be explicitly to give the patient the option of taking her own life; or it might be more ambiguous. ("Don't take all of them or it could kill you.") Do we want dying patients to have such information and choice, or should we perhaps protect them from themselves by depriving them of potent medication that might be used to take their own lives? It is very difficult to prosecute doctors successfully in the face of such ambiguity, especially if they are clearly motivated by compassion for their terminally ill patients rather than self-interest.

"Medical ethics do not allow me to assist in your death. I am, however, permitted to keep you miserable as long as possible."

© Peter Steiner. Reprinted with permission.

Many dying patients often have potentially lethal doses of medication at home that are being used to treat their symptoms. To withhold such medicine because of an abstract fear about suicide would be immoral, and in violation of fundamental principles of comfort care. Unfortunately, some physicians continue to undermedicate potentially treatable symptoms of dying patients, in part out of vague fears about patient suicide, but probably as significantly by their fear of legal or professional investigation should their patient take an overdose. If the patient is suffering from a reversible depression that is distorting her judgment, then caution and conservatism must be exercised until the distortion is resolved. Yet undertreating a dying patient's symptoms because of unsubstantiated fears about liability is unfortunately quite legal, though clearly unethical and immoral.

ASSISTED SUICIDE AND THE LAW

There are laws in thirty-six states, including New York State where I practice, prohibiting assisted suicide. The intent of these laws is presumably to prohibit persons from promoting a suicide for malicious intent, for example, by giving a loaded gun to a rich relative who is experiencing transient depression. No physician or family member has ever been convicted of assisting in the suicide of a severely ill patient with intractable suffering. Such acts appear to be looked upon by juries as acts of compassion not intended to be covered by the law. Yet the laws exist, and the threat of professional or legal repercussions is severe enough to prohibit many doctors from assisting their patients even when they consider the patients' requests rational and compelling. These laws perpetuate and exaggerate the power differences between vulnerable patients and their physicians, and put patients' fates more than ever at the discretion of their physicians.

In physician-assisted suicide, the patient commits the final act herself. The physician's participation is indirect, and there can always be a reasonable doubt about the intention as long as the prescribed drug has other medicinal uses. My patient, Diane, felt she had to be alone at her death in order to maintain this legal ambiguity, and to protect her family and me should her act ever be discovered. No one should have to be alone at death to protect anyone. Ironically and tragically, my innocence in the eyes of the grand jury, which investigated my involvement with Diane in response to the article [in the March 7, 1991, New England Journal of Medicine], was determined in no small measure by the fact that I was not present at her death. Laws that indirectly promote loneliness and abandonment at death should be carefully reconsidered to ensure that they don't have the unintended effect of further isolating and disempowering rather than protecting the dying person.

Euthanasia is defined as the act of painlessly putting to death a person who is suffering from an incurable, painful disease or condition. Its definition suggests a quiet and easy death—a "good death." Euthanasia is equated by some with "mercy killing," and its mention raises worries about involuntary killing and progressive disregard for human life. For others, the images of a painless escape from extreme suffering into death offer the promise of more compassionate and humane options for the dying. Unlike assisted suicide, where the legal implications have yet to be fully clarified, euthanasia is illegal in all states in the United States and likely to be vigorously prosecuted. It is also illegal in all other countries, though in the Netherlands it is explicitly left unprosecuted provided that specific guidelines are met.

"VOLUNTARY" AND "INVOLUNTARY" EUTHANASIA

Several distinctions are of critical importance in a serious discussion about euthanasia. The first is "voluntary" versus "involuntary," and the second is "active" versus "passive." "Voluntary" euthanasia means that the act of putting the person to death is the end result of the person's own free will. Consideration of voluntary euthanasia as an option, and the request for its use, must emanate from the patient *and no one else*. The patient's rational thought processes must not be distorted by depression or other sources of cognitive impairment. Unlike assisted suicide, where the physician provides the means for the patient to subsequently use, in euthanasia the physician is the direct agent of death. Although voluntary euthanasia can potentially be as humane and morally justifiable as assisted suicide, it puts the physician in a very powerful position. Many physicians and policy makers feel great trepidation because of the potential for abuse (e.g., physician-initiated euthanasia on incompetent patients or in ambiguous situations) or error (e.g., the patient changing her mind at the last minute).

"Involuntary" euthanasia means that the person is put to death without explicitly requesting it. Although this could be an act motivated by compassion for a severely suffering, incompetent patient, there is too much subjectivity and personal variation in the definition of "suffering" to condone such "acts of mercy." Involuntary euthanasia could also be used for completely immoral purposes—for example, on incompetent or even competent persons as an act of eugenics and social manipulation. Such abuses were witnessed in Nazi Germany, as we should never forget. Involuntary euthanasia, even when compassionately motivated, should remain criminal, and should be vigorously prosecuted and prohibited.

Involuntary euthanasia is a fundamentally different act both morally and ethically from responding to a voluntary request for euthanasia by a competent patient who has no escape from his suffering other than death. Voluntary euthanasia is an area worthy of our serious consideration, since it would allow patients who have exhausted all other reasonable options to choose death rather than continue suffering. Involuntary euthanasia, even when compassionately motivated, is extremely dangerous ground because of the inevitable subjectivity and personal variation of human suffering, and because of the potential for social abuse when one starts making such profound decisions on behalf of other persons who cannot express their own wishes. Perhaps fully competent suffering persons should be given the possibility of making such decisions for themselves; but under no circumstances should we allow such decisions to be made on behalf of those who are incompetent.

"ACTIVE" AND "PASSIVE" EUTHANASIA

The distinction between "active" and "passive" euthanasia rests upon the assumption that it is ethically permissible for physicians to withhold or withdraw life-sustaining medical treatment at the patient's request, and let the patient die passively of "natural causes." Such "passive" euthanasia is based on the fundamental ethical principle that informed, autonomous patients have the right to refuse any and all medical treatments, no matter what the consequences. Yet, under circumstances of identical or even greater suffering where no life-sustaining treatment is being used, current law forbids the physician to take direct action designed to achieve the same end—even if it is rationally requested by the patient and would result in a more humane death. Passive euthanasia, along with the double effect of narcotic pain medicine, probably accounts for the vast majority of the estimated six thousand planned deaths in United States hospitals each day. How many times lines are secretly crossed and distinctions blurred in the care of these dying patients is simply not known.

AN IMPORTANT DISTINCTION

Some ethicists believe that there is a fundamentally important distinction between active and passive euthanasia. Death is the intended outcome in both circumstances, but the physicians' actions are directly causal in active euthanasia, whereas it is the physicians' "inaction" in passive euthanasia that allows the patient to die of "natural causes." By maintaining this distinction, the medical profession allegedly remains untainted by becoming an agent of death. Yet, in the cloudy world of patient care, these distinctions can become more illusory than real, and our attempts to remain ethically pure sometimes extract a considerable price from dying persons who have little left to give. The intent of both active and passive euthanasia is to finally allow the patient with no other good options to die in the most humane way possible.

ETHICS AND TRUST

The highest ethical imperative of doctors should be to provide care in whatever way best serves patients' interests, in accord with each patient's wishes, not with a theoretical commitment to preserve life no matter what the cost in suffering. If a patient requests help with suicide and the doctor believes the request is appropriate, requiring someone else to provide the assistance would be a form of abandonment. Doctors who are opposed in principle need not assist, but they should make their patients aware of their position early in the relationship so that a patient who chooses to select another doctor can do so. The greatest harm we can do is to consign a desperate patient to unbearable suffering—or force the patient to seek out a stranger like Dr. Kevorkian. Contrary to the frequent assertion that permitting physician-assisted suicide would lead patients to distrust their doctors, I believe distrust is more likely to arise from uncertainty about whether a doctor will honor a patient's wishes.

Marcia Angell, *New England Journal of Medicine*, January 2, 1997.

One does not need to have a great deal of medical experience to find an example of passive euthanasia resulting in a very difficult death from "natural causes." Take for example a patient with end-stage, metastatic lung cancer who is near death from respiratory failure. He has tried to prolong his life through chemotherapy and radiation, but is now losing weight, extremely short of breath, and nearing the end of the road. He has elected to forgo cardiopulmonary resuscitation and mechanical ventilation (breathing machine) and knows that his death is inevitable. In fact, he has even begun to look forward to death as an escape from his life, which now feels completely empty, devoid of future or hope. So far, most physicians and ethicists would be comfortable with this example of passive euthanasia, allowing the person to die "naturally" of respiratory failure rather than prolonging his death by putting him on a mechanical ventilator.

Yet suppose that this patient has an overwhelming fear of suffocation, and wants to go to sleep quickly and not wake up, rather than continuing the agony of gradual suffocation for days or even weeks prior to his inevitable death. His request is confirmed to be rational, and his family agrees that he should be spared this final struggle if at all possible. Since there is no life-sustaining treatment to discontinue, passive euthanasia does not provide help or guidance at this point. According to comfort care principles, his shortness of breath can be treated with narcotics in doses intended to limit the feelings of discomfort, but not to intentionally produce death. His shortness of breath and feelings of extreme anxiety are therefore treated with an infusion of morphine until he falls asleep and appears relaxed. Yet periodically he awakens, thrashing and screaming from a terrifying feeling of suffocation. His morphine dose is appropriately increased to the point that he is relaxed enough to again lose consciousness, and no further. Unfortunately, a primitive drive to continue breathing sustains him whenever he drifts off into sleep. He alternates between periods of extreme agitation and a medicated sleep on the edge of death, where he lingers for over a week on gradually increasing doses of morphine before finally succumbing. Anyone who has witnessed such "natural deaths" cannot help but be troubled by their nightmarish quality.

An Escape from Suffering

The option of a physician-assisted death, whether by assisted suicide or active voluntary euthanasia, would allow patients such as this an escape from meaningless torment prior to death. When death is the only way to relieve suffering, and inevitable regardless, why not allow it to come in the most humane and dignified way possible? Why is it considered ethical to die of "natural causes" after a long heroic fight against illness filled with "unnatural" life-prolonging medical interventions, and unethical to allow patients to take charge at the end of a long illness and choose to die painlessly and quickly? Most of us hope to be fortunate enough to experience a "good death" when we have to die, and to be spared an agonizing ordeal at the very end. Many of us hope that if we do end up in such unfortunate circumstances, we can find a physician who will help us creatively explore all possibilities, including facilitating a relatively quick and painless death. Hopefully we will never need it, but the possibility would be very reassuring.

| "Suicide, when viewed objectively, is a
| gravely immoral act."

ASSISTED SUICIDE IS IMMORAL

John Paul II

In the following viewpoint, John Paul II, the pope of the Roman Catholic Church, contends that assisted suicide and euthanasia are immoral acts because only God has the right to end a life. Every human being has a sacred and inviolable right to life, he maintains. True compassion for an ill person's suffering should be shown through companionship and support, he argues, not by helping the sufferer to die.

As you read, consider the following questions:

1. How does euthanasia differ from forgoing aggressive medical treatment, according to John Paul II?
2. In the pope's view, why is palliative care that shortens a life permissible?
3. What is St. Augustine's opinion concerning assisted suicide, as cited by the author?

From Pope John Paul II's encyclical *Evangelium Vitae* as it appeared in *Origins*, the official organ of the U.S. National Council of Catholic Bishops, April 6, 1995.

"It is I who bring both death and life." (*Deuteronomy* 32:39)

At the end of life's spectrum, men and women find themselves facing the mystery of death. Today, as a result of advances in medicine and in a cultural context frequently closed to the transcendent, the experience of dying is marked by new features. When the prevailing tendency is to value life only to the extent that it brings pleasure and well-being, suffering seems like an unbearable setback, something from which one must be freed at all costs. Death is considered "senseless" if it suddenly interrupts a life still open to a future of new and interesting experiences. But it becomes a "rightful liberation" once life is held to be no longer meaningful because it is filled with pain and inexorably doomed to even greater suffering.

Furthermore, when he denies or neglects his fundamental relationship to God, man thinks he is his own rule and measure, with the right to demand that society should guarantee him the ways and means of deciding what to do with his life in full and complete autonomy. It is especially people in the developed countries who act in this way: They feel encouraged to do so also by the constant progress of medicine and its ever more advanced techniques. By using highly sophisticated systems and equipment, science and medical practice today are able not only to attend to cases formerly considered untreatable and to reduce or eliminate pain, but also to sustain and prolong life even in situations of extreme frailty, to resuscitate artificially patients whose basic biological functions have undergone sudden collapse and to use special procedures to make organs available for transplanting.

In this context the temptation grows to have recourse to euthanasia, that is, to take control of death and bring it about before its time, "gently" ending one's own life or the life of others. In reality what might seem logical and humane, when looked at more closely is seen to be senseless and inhumane. Here we are faced with one of the more alarming symptoms of the "culture of death," which is advancing above all in prosperous societies, marked by an attitude of excessive preoccupation with efficiency, and which sees the growing number of elderly and disabled people as intolerable and too burdensome. These people are very often isolated by their families and by society, which are organized almost exclusively on the basis of criteria of productive efficiency, according to which a hopelessly impaired life no longer has any value.

For a correct moral judgment on euthanasia, in the first place a clear definition is required. Euthanasia in the strict sense is understood to be an action or omission which of itself and by intention causes death, with the purpose of eliminating all suffering. According to the 1980 Congregation for the Doctrine of the Faith, Declaration on Euthanasia, *Jura et Bona II*, "Euthanasia's terms of reference, therefore, are to be found in the intention of the will and in the methods used."

Euthanasia must be distinguished from the decision to forgo so-called "aggressive medical treatment," in other words, medical procedures which no longer correspond to the real situation of the patient either because they are by now disproportionate to any expected results or because they impose an excessive burden on the patient and his family. In such situations, when death is clearly imminent and inevitable, the Declaration on Euthanasia states that one can in conscience "refuse forms of treatment that would only secure a precarious and burdensome prolongation of life, so long as the normal care due to the sick person in similar cases is not interrupted." Certainly there is a moral obligation to care for oneself and to allow oneself to be cared for, but this duty must take account of concrete circumstances. It needs to be determined whether the means of treatment available are objectively proportionate to the prospects for improvement. To forgo extraordinary or disproportionate means is not the equivalent of suicide or euthanasia; it rather expresses acceptance of the human condition in the face of death.

PALLIATIVE CARE

In modern medicine, increased attention is being given to what are called "methods of palliative care," which seek to make suffering more bearable in the final stages of illness and to ensure that the patient is supported and accompanied in his or her ordeal. Among the questions which arise in this context is that of the licitness of using various types of painkillers and sedatives for relieving the patient's pain when this involves the risk of shortening life. While praise may be due to the person who voluntarily accepts suffering by forgoing treatment with painkillers in order to remain fully lucid and, if a believer, to share consciously in the Lord's passion, such "heroic" behavior cannot be considered the duty of everyone. Pius XII affirmed that it is licit to relieve pain by narcotics even when the result is decreased consciousness and a shortening of life, "if no other means exist, and if, in the given circumstances, this does not prevent the carrying out of other religious and moral duties." In such a case, death is not willed or sought, even though for reasonable motives one runs the risk of it: There is simply a desire to ease pain effectively by using the analgesics which medicine provides. All the same, "it is not right to deprive the dying person of consciousness without a serious reason": As they approach death people ought to be able to satisfy their moral and family duties, and above all they ought to be able to prepare in a fully conscious way for their definitive meeting with God.

Moral Wisdom

Human community and the entirety of civilization is premised upon a relationship of moral claims and duties between persons. Personhood has no meaning apart from life. If life is a thing that can be renounced or taken at will, the moral structure of human community, understood as a community of persons, is shattered. Whatever the intentions of their proponents, proposals for legalizing euthanasia must be seen not as a solution to discrete problems but as an assault upon the fundamental ideas undergirding the possibility of moral order. The alternative to that moral order is the lethal disorder of a brave new world in which killing is defined as caring, life is viewed as the enemy, and death is counted as a benefit to be bestowed.

The Ramsey Colloquium, *First Things*, February 1992.

Taking into account these distinctions, in harmony with the magisterium of my predecessors and in communion with the bishops of the Catholic Church, I confirm that *euthanasia is a grave violation of the law of God*, since it is the deliberate and morally unacceptable killing of a human person. This doctrine is based upon the natural law and upon the written word of God, is transmitted by the church's tradition and taught by the ordinary and universal magisterium.

Depending on the circumstances, this practice involves the malice proper to suicide or murder.

Suicide is always as morally objectionable as murder. The church's tradition has always rejected it as a gravely evil choice. Even though a certain psychological, cultural and social conditioning may induce a person to carry out an action which so radically contradicts the innate inclination to life, thus lessening or removing subjective responsibility, suicide, when viewed objectively, is a gravely immoral act. In fact, it involves the rejection of love of self and the renunciation of the obligation of justice and charity toward one's neighbor, toward the communities to which one belongs and toward society as a whole. In its deepest reality, suicide represents a rejection of God's absolute sovereignty over life and death as proclaimed in the prayer of the ancient sage of Israel: "You have power over life and death; you lead men down to the gates of Hades and back again" (Wisdom of Solomon 16:13; cf. Tobit 13:2).

ASSISTED SUICIDE CAN NEVER BE EXCUSED

To concur with the intention of another person to commit suicide and to help in carrying it out through so-called "assisted suicide" means to cooperate in and at times to be the actual perpetrator of an injustice which can never be excused even if it is requested. In a remarkably relevant passage, St. Augustine writes that "it is never licit to kill another: even if he should wish it, indeed if he request it because, hanging between life and death, he begs for help in freeing the soul struggling against the bonds of the body and longing to be released; nor is it licit even when a sick person is no longer able to live." Even when not motivated by a selfish refusal to be burdened with the life of someone who is suffering, euthanasia must be called a false mercy and indeed a disturbing "perversion" of mercy. True "compassion" leads to sharing another's pain; it does not kill the person whose suffering we cannot bear. Moreover, the act of euthanasia appears all the more perverse if it is carried out by those like relatives, who are supposed to treat a family member with patience and love, or by those such as doctors, who by virtue of their specific profession are supposed to care for the sick person even in the most painful terminal stages.

The choice of euthanasia becomes more serious when it takes the form of a murder committed by others on a person who has in no way requested it and who has never consented to it. The height of arbitrariness and injustice is reached when certain people such as physicians or legislators arrogate to themselves the power to decide who ought to live and who ought to die. Once again we find ourselves before the temptation of Eden: to become like God, who "knows good and evil" (cf. Genesis 3:5). God alone has the power over life and death: "It is I who bring both death and life" (Deuteronomy 32:39; cf. 2 Kings 5:7; 1 Samuel 2:6). But he only exercises this power in accordance with a plan of wisdom and love. When man usurps this power, being enslaved by a foolish and selfish way of thinking, he inevitably uses it for injustice and death. Thus the life of the person who is weak is put into the hands of the one who is strong; in society the sense of justice is lost, and mutual trust, the basis of every authentic interpersonal relationship, is undermined at its root.

A REQUEST FOR COMPANIONSHIP AND SUPPORT

Quite different from this is the way of love and true mercy, which our common humanity calls for and upon which faith in Christ the Redeemer, who died and rose again, sheds ever new light. The request which arises from the human heart in the supreme confrontation with suffering and death, especially when faced with the temptation to give up in utter desperation, is above all a request for companionship, sympathy and support in the time of trial. It is a plea for help to keep on hoping when all human hopes fail. As the Second Vatican Council reminds us: "It is in the face of death that the riddle of human existence becomes most acute" and yet "man rightly follows the intuition of his heart when he abhors and repudiates the absolute ruin and total disappearance of his own person. Man rebels against death because he bears in himself an eternal seed which cannot be reduced to mere matter."

KILLING THE SICK AND ELDERLY

If we acknowledge the sacredness of human life and the reality of God-given rights and corresponding duties, we must acknowledge that the elderly, handicapped and unborn babies possess intrinsic moral worth, dignity, value and significance. Therefore, euthanasia, physician-assisted suicide and infanticide are morally wrong, because even an elderly or handicapped person of "no use" to society nevertheless is a human being with intrinsic moral worth and dignity.

Haven Bradford Gow, *Conservative Review*, March/April 1995.

This natural aversion to death and this incipient hope of immortality are illumined and brought to fulfillment by Christian faith, which both promises and offers a share in the victory of the risen Christ: It is the victory of the one who by his redemptive death has set man free from death, "the wages of sin" (Romans 6:23), and has given him the Spirit, the pledge of resurrection and of life (cf. Romans 8:11). The certainty of future immortality and hope in the promised resurrection cast new light on the mystery of suffering and death, and fill the believer with an extraordinary capacity to trust fully in the plan of God.

THE SUPREME ACT OF OBEDIENCE

The apostle Paul expressed this newness in terms of belonging completely to the Lord, who embraces every human condition: "None of us lives to himself, and none of us dies to himself. If we live, we live to the Lord, and if we die, we die to the Lord; so then, whether we live or whether we die, we are the Lord's" (Romans 14:7–8). Dying to the Lord means experiencing one's death as the supreme act of obedience to the Father (cf. Philippians 2:8), being ready to meet death at the "hour" willed and chosen by him (cf. John 13:1), which can only mean when one's earthly pilgrimage is completed. Living to the Lord also means recognizing that suffering, while still an evil and a trial in itself, can always become a source of good. It becomes such if it is experienced for love and with love through sharing, by God's gracious gift and one's own personal and free choice, in the suffering of Christ crucified. In this way the person who lives his suffering in the Lord grows more fully conformed to him (cf. Philippians 3:10; 1 Peter 2:21) and more closely associated with his redemptive work on behalf of the church and humanity. This was the experience of St. Paul, which every person who suffers is called to relive: "I rejoice in my sufferings for your sake, and in my flesh I complete what is lacking in Christ's afflictions for the sake of his body, that is, the church" (Colossians 1:24).

> "Killing [a] patient, no matter what
> the law says or what the
> circumstances are, is still killing."

PHYSICIAN-ASSISTED SUICIDE IS MURDER

Walter Reich

In the following viewpoint, Walter Reich argues that doctors who help their patients commit suicide are guilty of murder. A doctor's role is to preserve life, he asserts, not to end it. He contends that if physicians are allowed to kill their patients, society will be likely to accept other immoral practices. Reich, a psychiatrist, is a senior scholar at the Woodrow Wilson International Center for Scholars and the director of the U.S. Holocaust Memorial Museum in Washington, D.C. The views expressed in this viewpoint are solely those of the author.

As you read, consider the following questions:

1. According to Reich, what rules do Dutch doctors have to follow in order to help their patients commit suicide?
2. What types of killings can society experience without losing moral decency, in Reich's opinion?
3. Where might the Netherlands' law permitting physician-assisted suicide have the greatest impact, in the author's view?

From "Mercy Killing Is Still Killing, and It Corrupts the Value of Life" by Walter Reich, *San Diego Union-Tribune*, March 2, 1993. Reprinted with permission.

In 1993, the Parliament of the Netherlands, one of the most humane nations on earth, gave Dutch physicians, members of one of the most humane professions on earth, permission to kill their patients.

Physicians still have to follow rules. The patient must ask for death, must not be depressed when asking for it, must be well informed about his illness and options and must feel his suffering is unacceptable.

The physician must consult a colleague before doing the deed and, having done it, must inform the authorities why he was justified in doing it.

DEATHS MAY SKYROCKET

In 1990, 1 out of 50 deaths in the Netherlands was the result of mercy killings carried out in a country in which ever more physicians were prepared to perform euthanasia and in which the authorities did not enforce existing laws against it.

In 1992, the number of such killings rose markedly; now it may skyrocket.

You don't have to be religious to mourn the new law. All you have to be is human and alive.

All you have to understand is that a patient, no matter how ill or despondent, is still human and still alive, and that killing that patient, no matter what the law says or what the circumstances are, is still killing.

People kill without benefit of the law every day. Soldiers kill other soldiers legally. But societies can experience such killings and remain essentially decent.

It's when they legalize the killings of their own innocent members that they remove an obstacle that blocks the all-too-easy slide of civilization into moral chaos. When they permit killing by medical means, they eviscerate the human essence of the medical enterprise.

Is the Netherlands about to join Nazi Germany by sliding into the hell of Auschwitz? Hardly. Members of the Parliament who voted for the mercy killing bill did so out of powerful feelings of compassion for patients.

A TROUBLING ACT

It's precisely because the Dutch have so exemplary a history of decency, and their parliamentarians so thorough a commitment to democracy, that the act is so troubling.

It provides a model for the easing by a democratic nation of the taboo against the legalized killing of innocent people—an easing girded by rules that seem tight now but that will be loosened, inevitably, in practice.

The spectacle of the formalized and regular killing of such patients—resulting not in 1 Dutch death out of 50 but in 5 deaths out of 50, or 10, or 20, or even more—will have a corrupting effect, not only on the value of life in the Netherlands but also in every other democratic country.

Mike Benson. Reprinted by special permission from United Features Syndicate.

But the greatest impact of this spectacle may be in undemocratic countries where authorities less humane than Dutch legislators may seize upon the Dutch example as a useful model without bothering to set up rules to guide physicians in their killing work.

They may even provide rules that permit, encourage or even demand all kinds of killing, beginning with the killing of people who ask for it and progressing to the killing of people who are said to deserve it.

An Oath to Preserve Life

Doctors in the Netherlands, like doctors everywhere, are bound by millennia of solemn oaths to preserve life. Their patients expect that commitment from them and the physicians expect it from themselves.

To be sure, it's a commitment that can get out of hand: Sometimes physicians preserve life artificially and mindlessly in a manner that, solely because of the work of machines, keeps the heart beating long after the brain has died.

But going overboard, when it's done out of a genuine desire to preserve life if even the smallest chance of recovery is possible, is an essentially noble act that, even if it is excessive, at least guards the central and classical values of medicine.

A CHANGING ROLE

However, once the medical commitment to life is undermined by legal sanction—once doctors trained to preserve life are no longer afraid of initiating death—then the very nature of the medical enterprise, and the very identity of the physician, is changed.

The doctor loses the mission of caring for life and takes on the role of an amoral medical technician—one whose duty could just as well be to end life as to preserve it.

That's a profession of which I want no part. Society deserves better. Physicians deserve better. And, most important of all, patients deserve better.

| "The nub is not whether physicians should kill, for in the technical sense we do, but rather whether euthanasia is justifiable killing."

PHYSICIAN-ASSISTED SUICIDE IS JUSTIFIABLE KILLING

Thomas A. Preston

Thomas A. Preston argues in the following viewpoint that the verb "to kill" merely means "to deprive of life" and should not necessarily have negative connotations. While doctors who practice assisted suicide do indeed "kill" their patients, Preston asserts, these doctors are not murderers because they do not act with evil intent. Furthermore, he contends that there is no ethical distinction between allowing a patient to die and assisted suicide; both are killing, he maintains. Preston is a doctor and professor of medicine at the University of Washington in Seattle.

As you read, consider the following questions:

1. What is incorrect about Daniel Callahan's argument that legalization of euthanasia will lead to the "right" of physicians to kill, according to Preston?
2. In the author's view, why is allowing a patient to die not considered a form of killing?
3. What could the resident who wrote "It's Over, Debbie" have done to avoid the appearance of intentionally killing the patient, according to Preston?

From Thomas A. Preston, "Professional Norms and Physician Attitudes Toward Euthanasia," *Journal of Law, Medicine & Ethics*, vol. 22, no. 1 (1994), pp. 36–40. References in the original article have been omitted here. Reprinted by permission.

The chair of the ethics committee of a major medical center agonized over how he, as a physician, and his organization should deal with Initiative 119, which, if passed, would legalize physician involvement in active, voluntary euthanasia in Washington State. [The initiative did not pass.] In the end, he said, he could not vote for aid-in-dying because "However much I want to reduce suffering, I myself just couldn't do it to one of my patients." He spoke of a personal distaste for the potential act, of a profound desire not to have to do it. It was not an ethical argument, but an honest and compelling expression of feelings. . . .

A major argument for physician opposition to aid-in-dying is the general prohibition against killing. Active, voluntary euthanasia is killing, but only within a very narrowly defined sense. Lexicographers define "to kill" as: "to deprive of life" without condition. "To kill" merely states a general fact. Thus, one is killed by a falling tree, or by a stroke, or by a person. "To deprive of life" implies an act, or the omission of a life-saving act, but makes no judgment as to whether the killing is intended, desired, or involves another person.

DEFINING "TO KILL"

The verb "to kill" is quite insufficient to describe euthanasia, from any perspective. We simply do not have a word in the English language up to the task of defining it. Nevertheless, opponents of euthanasia favor the word because of its pervasive implication of impropriety, wantonness, or even evil intent. To wit, in the twenty-three-sentence "Statement Against" Initiative 119 in the 1991 Washington State Voters Pamphlet, "kill" or "killing" appeared eight times, and "homicide" was used twice. In a thirty-second spot commercial, former Surgeon General C. Everett Koop said that Initiative 119 would allow doctors to kill the poor, the weak, and the aged. Proponents of the initiative avoided the word "kill" and used "aid-in-dying" or "death with dignity."

An extension of the term killing, used to solidify the implication of wantonness or criminality of the act, is the charge that legalized euthanasia would give physicians the "right" to kill. Daniel Callahan argues that "killings authorized in the name of mercy . . . give one person an absolute power over another," and also asks, "How are we to make the moral move from my right of self-determination to some doctor's right to kill me—from my right to his right?" Alexander Morgan Capron says "the decision to perform active euthanasia is one that proclaims the omnipotence (and omniscience) of health care professionals."

These arguments are not correct, because a "right" in the social and legal sense does not derive from the arbitrary wish or approval of the person acting. No physician has a right to put a patient "to sleep," nor is this a part of any euthanasia proposal. The legal and ethical basis by which a physician may do any procedure on a patient, or an automobile mechanic may fix a car, comes from the request and consent of the patient or the automobile owner, and is not an inherent right of the physician or mechanic.

A HEROIC ACT

Far from being a cowardly act, suicide is heroic when death is viewed as a part of life, a terminal end of the great circle. Logic and fairness dictate an extension of the right [to choose the course of their medical treatment] to all categories of patients, the dying, the chronically ill and those in a persistent vegetative state. For physicians not to help their patients die, if dying is that patient's considered choice, is, in my view, the act of cowardice. When the existential experience of dying becomes an affront to the patient's own definition of life, when the suffering of the conscious terminally ill or chronically ill patient experience goes far beyond physical pain, it is this anguish, this degrading loss of control with which we must deal. American physicians must be prepared to extend their ethic, to meet death with their patients. This would contribute to the physician's stature as healer, not diminish it.

Ralph E. Dittman, *Priorities*, Spring 1992.

The use of the word "kill" is an etymological liberty based on linguistic inadequacy, and physicians mold usage of the word to exclude it from normative medical practices while applying it to practices they dislike, as with euthanasia, for example. The concept that "physicians must not kill" is not, in praxis, viable; physicians *do kill*, inadvertently through complications of procedures or drugs, in cases of death due to negligence, and even intentionally, as by withdrawal of life-supporting treatment and through the "double effect." The nub is not whether physicians should kill, for in the technical sense we do, but rather whether euthanasia is justifiable killing.

WITHDRAWAL OF LIFE-SUSTAINING TREATMENT

Withdrawal of life-sustaining treatment is an active step that allows death to ensue. In 1975, the father of Karen Ann Quinlan filed suit to remove her ventilator, and the following day the local newspaper ran the headline "Father Wants to Kill Daughter." Today, withdrawal of life-sustaining treatment is good and legal medical practice, and physicians do not call it killing. However, were a spouse to disconnect the ventilator of a terminally ill and suffering patient who was begging to die, we might call the act killing. Regardless of intent or propriety, or who does it, the act deprives someone of life, and so constitutes killing. The distinction is not in the act, but in the norms of professionally acceptable behavior.

The common method of deluding ourselves into thinking we are not killing when we withdraw life-sustaining treatment is the notion of "allowing the patient to die." As Leon R. Kass puts it, "Not the physician, but the underlying fatal illness becomes the true cause of death." Of course, the underlying illness is the cause of death, but, when the patient dies, the doctor nevertheless has killed by his act. Regardless of intent, "allowing to die" is a descriptive term used to connote professional approval of a form of killing.

The key to rationalization of withdrawal of life-sustaining treatment as "allowing to die" rather than killing is the passage of time, or the speed with which the patient dies. The physician who withdraws life-sustaining treatment does not intend immediate death following her act, for such would constitute evident euthanasia. But neither does the physician intend prolongation of life, otherwise she would not withdraw life-sustaining treatment. The passage of time, if only a few minutes, is requisite for the appearance of natural death and the absolution of the physician. But semantic exercises about the mode of death and intent do not nullify the act of killing, however inadequate and falsely negative the word may be in describing this humane practice.

THE "DOUBLE EFFECT"

Perhaps the most egregious professional delusion about the true nature of an act involves the so-called "double effect" of allegedly unintended death due to administration of a narcotic to relieve pain. The relatively few cases in which death is not expected but incidental to drug suppression of pain provide the pretext for physicians' claims of nonintentional death using the double effect.

In this transformation of technical killing into an acceptable medical act, we displace by time and stated intent the expected and accepted end, which is death. As with withdrawal of life-sustaining treatment, we extend the injections, or the pills, over hours or days, and so we and all observers may say that death was unintended. Were the physician to administer a single lethal injection of a narcotic for the purpose of "pain relief," observers would be forced to call the act euthanasia.

Consider the case of the anonymous resident who wrote "It's Over, Debbie" [a 1988 article in the *Journal of the American Medical Association*]. This young physician reported giving a lethal injection of morphine to a woman suffering from terminal cancer whom she, the resident, had never met. Willard Gaylin and his co-authors correctly call the act a "killing," and point out that the resident may not have known the patient well enough to make such a decision. But the crux of the condemnation is this: because "he gives her a lethal injection of morphine," the resident "clearly intend[s] the death that promptly ensues." The open admission of intent violates the professional taboo, but I submit that the reaction in this case is not because the injection was lethal, but because death ensued *promptly*.

Why so? The resident was inexperienced. Suppose that the intent had been exactly the same; but, instead of injecting 20 mg of morphine all at once, suppose she began a low-dose morphine drip and increased the rate of infusion of the drug over the next hour or more until the patient died. Had the resident informed the woman that the treatment would put an end to her suffering but carried the risk of arresting her breathing, and then written the same anonymous account with the exception of this difference in the duration of the infusion, the article might not have provoked enough interest to merit publication. But, had it been published anyway, it would have passed as an ethically acceptable act because it would fall within professional norms. Either way, it is killing.

PHYSICIANS HAVE KILLED

From Hippocrates to the hypocrisy of the "double effect," physicians have, by the strict definition, killed patients to relieve suffering. The confounding professional difference between euthanasia, which physicians decry, and withdrawal of life-supporting treatment and the "double effect," which they accept, is not "killing," but normative acceptance of the latter two medical practices.

The question whether and when physicians should intentionally end life deserves full and continued debate, but physicians first must honestly acknowledge two aspects of present practice: our widespread participation in intentional end-of-life actions, and the prominence of professional norms in how we define these practices. So long as physicians reject euthanasia as killing, without seeing it as one of many end-of-life practices that also kill but are not so called, they will be unable to bring reason and the needs of many of their patients to the issue.

PERIODICAL BIBLIOGRAPHY

The following articles have been selected to supplement the diverse views presented in this chapter. Addresses are provided for periodicals not indexed in the *Readers' Guide to Periodical Literature*, the *Alternative Press Index*, the *Social Sciences Index*, or the *Index to Legal Periodicals and Books*.

Marcia Angell	"The Supreme Court and Physician-Assisted Suicide—The Ultimate Right," *New England Journal of Medicine*, January 2, 1997. Available from 10 Shattuck St., Boston, MA 02115-6094.
Lisa Belkin	"There's No Simple Suicide," *New York Times Magazine*, November 14, 1993.
Peter J. Bernardi	"Coming Soon: Your Neighborhood T.S.C.," *America*, April 30, 1994.
Lisa Hobbs Birnie	"The Final Days," *Maclean's*, June 27, 1994.
Stephen L. Carter	"Rush to a Lethal Judgment," *New York Times Magazine*, July 21, 1996.
Barbara Dority	"In the Hands of the People," *Humanist*, July/August 1996.
Ronald Dworkin	"Sex, Death, and the Courts," *New York Review of Books*, August 8, 1996.
Tom Flynn	"A Case for Mercy Killing," *Free Inquiry*, Summer 1993. Available from PO Box 664, Amherst, NY 14226-0664.
Kathleen M. Foley	"Competent Care for the Dying Instead of Physician-Assisted Suicide," *New England Journal of Medicine*, January 2, 1997.
Steve Hallock	"Physician-Assisted Suicide: 'Slippery Slope' or Civil Right?" *Humanist*, July/August 1996.
Charles Krauthammer	"First and Last, Do No Harm," *Time*, April 15, 1996.
Joseph P. Shapiro	"Euthanasia's Home," *U.S. News & World Report*, January 13, 1997.
Wesley J. Smith	"There's No Such Thing As a Simple Suicide," *Human Life Review*, Winter 1994. Available from 150 E. 35th St., New York, NY 10016.
David Van Biema	"Is There a Right to Die?" *Time*, January 13, 1997.

CHAPTER 4

HOW CAN SUICIDE
BE PREVENTED?

Chapter Preface

The first suicide prevention center, the Save-a-Life League, was founded in 1906 in New York, the result of a meeting between minister Harry M. Warren and a suicidal young woman. After her suicide attempt, from which she later died, the woman told Warren, "I think maybe if I had talked to someone like you, I wouldn't have done it." Warren was spurred by the woman's words to organize a network of people who would be available to talk to anyone who was considering suicide.

The suicide prevention movement remained small until the 1960s, when suicide came to be seen as a social problem. Most of the two hundred secular suicide prevention centers now operating in the United States are affiliated with local mental health associations and depend on community donations. To boost monetary support, in their early years many of these centers offered high estimations of the number of lives they had saved. For example, the Save-a-Life League maintained that it saved one thousand lives a year in its first seventy-five years. However, this number was not corroborated by studies that showed no difference in suicide rates in cities with suicide prevention centers and without suicide prevention centers. These same studies found that the typical caller to a suicide hotline is a young or middle-aged female, while the typical suicide victim is an elderly white male.

Supporters of suicide prevention centers admit that previous claims of the number of lives saved may have been exaggerated, but they contend that the centers do help prevent suicides. According to George Howe Colt, author of *The Enigma of Suicide*, a study in Alabama found that suicides by young white females—the group to which most suicide hotline callers belong—were lower in counties with a suicide prevention center than in counties without a center. The study concluded that suicide prevention centers nationwide save the lives of 637 young white females each year.

Suicide hotlines are just one way that society tries to prevent suicide. The authors in the following chapter examine other means of suicide prevention.

I"Intervention is prevention."

INTERVENTION CAN PREVENT SUICIDE

Ralph L.V. Rickgarn

Ralph L.V. Rickgarn is the author of *Perspectives on College Student Suicide*, from which the following viewpoint is excerpted. He is also a suicide consultant and intervention trainer for elementary, secondary, and postsecondary schools. Rickgarn asserts that anyone can participate in suicide intervention. Suicide intervention begins with recognizing the signs of suicidal intent, he maintains. If friends or family members are able to recognize the danger signals of suicidal behavior in an individual and to take positive steps toward intervention, Rickgarn contends, they may be able to prevent that person from committing suicide.

As you read, consider the following questions:

1. What are the three levels of suicide intervention, according to Rickgarn?
2. Who is generally the first to become aware of suicidal clues, in the author's opinion?
3. Why is it important to use the word "suicide" during an intervention, in the author's opinion?

To intervene is to care! To intervene is to make a commitment! Can you do that? In fact, anyone can "intervene" but there is more to the process than that. In many ways, intervention can be compared to swimming in a lake. Some people arrive at the lake and gingerly touch their toe to the water to see if it is too cold. Others rush into the water and immediately dash for the shore again having experienced the direct effect of the water upon their bodies. Others rather methodically wade out and deliberately plunge into the water and swim for the raft and having reached it, pull themselves onto the raft and enjoy the sunlight. While it is possible that anyone can intervene with a suicidal person, there may be reasons why they should not do so. And this does not make that person any less caring or concerned. It is just that she or he has some issues in their own life that make it more appropriate for them to limit their intervention to helping the suicidal person reach another helper. . . .

LEVELS OF INTERVENTION

Intervention with a suicidal person is both very time consuming and very energy consuming. Therefore it is important to understand that there are different levels of intervention and to acknowledge which level is appropriate for our own action is crucial. Initially, anyone who wants to can begin an intervention when they detect that someone appears to be (or is) expressing suicidal ideas. I would call this the *every person* intervention level. The intervention at this level is to give permission to the person to talk about whatever there is in his or her life causing them to consider suicide. This is the development of a rapport and trust which communicates to the suicidal person that there is an empathic relationship and the intervener wants to facilitate the person's access to a more professional level of assistance.

At this level we need to be certain that we include students. Often it is the suicidal student's peers who become aware of his or her suicidal thoughts or impending actions. M.T. Lawrence and J.R. Ureda surveyed 1,131 university freshmen and found they were able to recognize suicidal behavior in their peers. The problem was they were either unsure or did not know how to make a helpful response. Programs can be developed to enable students to achieve a reasonable comfort level with their suicidal peers. This can be done through accurate information, skill training, modeling, and role playing. These activities can be offered on a volunteer level and will increase emotional comfort in situations that are stressful and emotional. The combination of knowledge and the belief that a person can take appropriate action is needed for effective intervention.

The second level I would call the *skilled helper* level. The previous intervener may accompany the suicidal person to an individual who has had training in para-professional counseling skills (e.g., a teacher, a resident assistant, a student affairs staff member) or who occupies a position where some formal training in counseling has taken place (e.g., a clergy person, a crisis line worker, a physician, a dentist, or a nurse). The intervention may begin at this level as the suicidal person seeks some assistance. For persons involved in the medical profession it is important to note that at least 50 percent of individuals who have committed suicide have sought medical attention within the previous six months. This has profound implications for the staff of college health services. Intervention at this level may provide some persons with the interaction they need to resolve their life situation, or they may be referred to persons at a third level.

The third level I would call the *professional* level. The interveners at this level are those persons who are professionally trained and include school counselors, social workers, psychologists, psychiatrists, and others who have had advanced training in counseling. Intervention at this level may involve outpatient counseling, medication, and hospitalization. Again, intervention at this level may begin through referrals or by initial contact with a suicidal person seeking resolution of a life problem. . . .

RECOGNIZING THE SIGNS

Intervention begins at any level with a recognition of a person's suicidal inclination. While this may be as obvious as someone coming directly to a person and asking for help, it is more likely that the intervener will have to be cognizant of the clues related to suicidal behavior. It is usually not mental health or other professionals who become aware of the potential risk of suicide. Rather, it is usually the suicidal person's peers, colleagues, friends, and family that become aware of the suicidal clues. This is precisely why it is very important to have programs for the general public on the recognition of the clues to suicidal behavior. These programs can assist in the elimination of attitudes of denial, teach people the clues to suicidal behavior and to recognize that all suicidal clues and threats should be taken seriously. Otherwise there is a genuine possibility that a significant clue may be avoided or missed and a suicide attempt or completed suicide may take place. Alan L. Berman and D.A. Jobes write, "Intervention in and the prevention of adolescent suicide often fundamentally depends on the awareness and sensitivity of key

people in the young person's life who seriously respond to obvious and veiled suicide clues and make referrals to those who
can help."

WHAT TO DO IF SOMEONE BECOMES SUICIDAL

Recently, I intervened to prevent a friend from committing suicide. My friend is alive and I have the satisfaction that I knew
what to do and had the opportunity to do it. That means a great
deal to me because I value my friend. . . .

Do take the signs [of suicide] seriously. If you don't feel equipped
to manage a crisis yourself, find another person to help you or
turn it over to someone you trust. Let the person's therapist know
you are worried and why. It's not a breach of confidentiality for
you to tell the therapist that you're worried about the behavior of
your friend. Though the therapist cannot talk about the person,
he or she can listen to you.

Remember, you would intervene if someone had a heart attack.
The suicidal impulse is just as deadly.

Elizabeth Lofgren, *Minnesota Depressive and Manic Depressive Association Newsletter*, March
1992.

There are a number of clues to suicidal ideation and action.
These may be behavioral, emotional or statements which are
made, indicating that the individual has some level of suicidal
risk. . . .

Many suicidal persons communicate their intentions by indirect methods. These indirect methods are used to determine if
anyone will take them seriously, if they really care, and if they
will take some action.

THE QUESTION TO ASK

"Are you thinking about committing suicide?" This is the question to ask. To do otherwise is to send someone searching for
another person who may hear his plea. The question will not
put the idea into someone's mind. That is the myth. Rather, it
will enable the person to speak of the intolerable situation that
has brought him or her to this point. This question is special in
two ways.

First of all, it doesn't avoid the issue. Interestingly, one of the
most common ways of responding to indications of suicidal
thoughts or behaviors is to ask, "You're not thinking of committing suicide are you?" There is an emphasis on the negative and
the communication given to the suicidal person is that the an-

swer that is desired is, "No, not me." And, that is more than likely the answer that will be given. It is apparent to the suicidal person that the responder is not desirous of entering into an interaction with him or her, for whatever reason. It has become apparent to me that regardless of other constriction(s) in their thinking, suicidal persons appear to be extremely capable of "reading" another person's intent. They are looking for a direct involvement not an indecisive possibility.

BE DIRECT

Second, this question says the word *suicide*. Some other responses are very ambiguous using euphemisms such as "hurting yourself," "doing harm" or even as ambiguous as "doing something to yourself." These responses communicate to the suicidal person that any involvement is tentative at best. For the suicidal person, the question becomes, "How much can I say before I will frighten you away?" Suicide is what we are talking about, the word "suicide" is what we need to say. It communicates clearly that we are willing to take a risk, that we are willing to engage in an intervention. Perhaps, most frightening of all, we are willing to take the risk of becoming a survivor. . . .

There are other actions that also need to be taken once the question has been asked and the response has been, "Yes." At this point, people are very concerned that they will do something that will "push the person over the edge" or make the matter much worse. A caring, empathic response and posture by an intervener will rarely produce a negative reaction. . . .

THE DO'S OF INTERVENTION

First and foremost, listen carefully to everything that is being said. Check out what you think you have heard. This not only indicates you *want* to understand what is being said, it also demonstrates you want to *understand* it accurately. It shows you care. If there are smoke screens, diversions or inconsistencies seek to have them clarified or gently challenge them. Listen to the words for context, content and affect, and observe the body language.

In the event you come upon someone who is suicidal and you do not know the person's name it is important to establish a connection by asking her or his name. You only need a first name to establish this very human linkage. This will demonstrate to the individual that you care enough to want to address her or him by name. Also tell the person your name so she or he can call you by name. This introduction is a very normal part of a human interaction and it lends some degree of normalcy to a stressful situation. Whatever the incident, using names is a powerful recognition of the individual as a distinct individual.

The focus of an intervention is upon the suicidal person. You want to find out as much as possible about them. Ask the person about themselves. Learn some basic information about where they live, their marital status, and other parts of their life. What is happening in their life at this time that would precipitate a suicidal behavior? Ask the person direct questions about the details of his or her planned action. Who is involved? What means are they planning to use? When are they planning to attempt/commit suicide? What has brought them to this decision? If possible, avoid questions that begin with the word, "Why?" "Why?" questions tend to have an accusatory sense for adolescents and young adults (probably for anybody) conjuring up a mental image of a parent or an authority figure saying, "Why did you do this?" These questions are important as they provide the basis for an assessment of suicidal risk. . . .

Assist the person in obtaining professional help by working with them to find a counselor. At colleges and universities there are usually mental health units whether they are part of the campus, as a health service, or an arrangement with a local medical or mental health facility. The individual may be very threatened by his or her emotional state and quite frightened at being out of control. Students may view the situation as representing yet another failure in their life, believing that they will be seen as incompetent. Therefore, it is extremely helpful to accompany the person to the counselor or doctor's office. They need support as they work to begin resolution of this life crisis. This action demonstrates a further caring for the individual at a time when they believe few if any people care what happens to them. . . .

PREVENTION BEGINS WITH EDUCATION

Intervention is prevention, the anticipating or countering in advance of a suicidal action. Prevention, consequently intervention, begins with education and training for all persons. These efforts could reduce the mythology and the apprehension that is present during an intervention and enable a greater number of persons to begin this process at the "every person" stage.

Interventions will only be as good as the knowledge that we have for understanding the diversity and the complexity of the risk factor matrix and the suicidal process. Interventions will only be as good as the people who are willing to engage their time and their energy in attempting to inhibit the suicidal process.

> "No one can ever be sure that a different choice [of action] would have prevented the suicide."

INTERVENTION MAY NOT PREVENT SUICIDE

Ann Smolin and John Guinan

In the following viewpoint, Ann Smolin and John Guinan contend that intervening in a suicide attempt may only postpone the suicide, not prevent it. They maintain that there is no way of knowing if a different course of action by the suicide survivors—the family and friends of a person who committed suicide—would have prevented the suicide. Smolin is a clinical social worker and the director of the Northern Westchester branch of the Westchester Jewish Community Services in New York. Guinan is a clinical psychologist and the director of the Wall Street Counseling Center, also in New York. They are the authors of *Healing After the Suicide of a Loved One*, a self-help book for suicide survivors, from which this viewpoint is excerpted.

As you read, consider the following questions:

1. In the authors' opinion, why do many suicide survivors feel guilty before a suicide occurs?
2. How is a suicide threat the ultimate form of blackmail, according to the authors?
3. Why, in Smolin and Guinan's opinion, are suicide survivors not responsible for causing a suicide?

The worst torture is thinking, "I could have done something to prevent it." Much of the talk in survivor support groups concerns the motivations of the suicide: "Why did he do it?" "What was she feeling?" "What could she have been thinking of?" While this questioning reflects a real wish to understand the feelings and motivations of the person who has killed himself in order to come to peace with the act, just as often it is an attempt to figure out what you, the survivor, could and should have done differently.

Survivors often believe, "If only I had stayed with him (or married him, or made love to him, or not insisted on moving to my own place, or . . .), he would still be alive." There is no way of knowing what would have happened. Even if you had done whatever it is you torment yourself for not doing, and even if you did deter the suicide from happening, that is hardly the same as preventing it altogether.

Take Off the Guilt-Colored Glasses

Deena came to our group after her daughter had killed herself. Her daughter had been quite depressed for some time, and Deena was spending a lot of time with her, trying to help her out of her depression. In our group, more than once, Deena discussed the nature of depression at some length and reviewed the onset of her daughter's depression. Deena castigated herself for not realizing the depth and the severity of her daughter's depression: "If only I had understood how depressed she was, and the seriousness of it, I would have had her hospitalized."

Eva's story was a far more effective reply to Deena's self-rebuke than anything a group facilitator might have said. Eva's daughter, like Deena's, had been depressed for a number of years, partly in reaction to her father's alcoholism, and partly, Eva felt, in response to Eva's own battle with cancer, which had gone on through much of her daughter's adolescence. Eva's daughter had been hospitalized. In fact, she was a patient in one of New York's better-known hospitals when she hung herself with the belt of the robe that the hospital gave her. (Eva did take note that in another hospital, where her daughter had been, patients were given robes without belts as a suicide precaution.)

Despite any lapse in judgment she might believe the hospital showed by providing her daughter with what became the immediate instrument of her suicide, Eva's most intense blaming was reserved for herself. Her self-accusation focused on her having been at fault in letting her daughter be hospitalized. With hindsight, Eva felt that she should have kept her daughter at home and spent more time with her, rather than heeding the psychiatrist's advice to distance herself from her daughter.

What added impact and poignancy to Deena and Eva's inventories of self-doubt was that they were delivered at the same survivor group meeting. Deena faulted herself for not having had her daughter hospitalized, while Eva regretted having agreed to let her daughter be hospitalized. Deena and Eva each felt that had they taken the opposite course, their daughters would still be alive.

NOTHING WOULD HAVE MADE A DIFFERENCE

My mom died more than 20 years ago when I was 16 and she was 49. She killed herself by mixing sleeping pills with alcohol. I remember the night with utter clarity.

My younger sister and I had returned home after playing evening basketball with friends. My father was reading the paper, my mother was in bed. I went to the bedside to see if she was resting or asleep for the night, and noticed that her breathing was strained and thick. I shook her shoulders, ordered her to wake up, slapped her cheeks. . . . She couldn't be roused. . . .

No death is easy. But suicide leaves a particular kind of discomfort. Distant acquaintances as well as loved ones feel compelled to solve the puzzle, searching for an explanation of what went wrong. Suicide notes are combed, analyzed, read between the lines. When, like my mother, the person leaves no note, an acute and hollow frustration remains. Lingering in people's faces, in the air of rooms where she once sat, in the twisting of each mind, is the same question: Is there anything I could have done to prevent this death? . . .

If my sister and I hadn't been playing basketball, if my brother hadn't been at a friend's house, if my dad hadn't been buried in the paper, could we have stopped her? Could we have helped?

The answer is no. I knew then, as I know more clearly now, that my mother was fighting a battle deeply within herself. . . . It was intensely personal, wrapped in contradictions and confusion, far from my reach. The inner workings of a person, the mysteries of the soul and psyche and personality, may exist in a private orbit, hidden, not in sync with the external world.

Katy Darby Rauch, *Washington Post*, May 17, 1994.

The common saying is that we all have 20/20 vision in hindsight, but this example of two survivors proves there are exceptions. The problem is that although you can see what you could have done differently before the suicide, it is not clear that you

could have permanently prevented a suicide from happening—
or even that it would have been prevented at that moment.

Had you taken an alternate course of action, maybe the suicide would have been put off until the next day, or the next
month, or even the next year. And, yes, if it had been put off,
maybe some more therapy or medication might have been attempted, and maybe the suicide really would have been averted
altogether. But maybe it could not have been—and there is no way of knowing! What it is possible to know is that whatever course you fault
yourself for not having taken, there is someone else blaming
himself for having taken that same course.

This is the immensely important lesson of Deena and Eva's
stories. No one can ever be sure that a different choice would
have prevented the suicide. Why convict yourself on the basis of
insufficient evidence when, indeed, no compelling evidence can
ever be obtained?

Paul laments having owned the gun with which his son shot
himself; he is right, of course, that if he had not owned a gun,
and had not kept it in his apartment, his son could not have shot
himself with it. But he could have taken an overdose of pills or
slashed his wrists. Yes, Paul may reply, but had he done one of
those things, we might have been able to get him to a hospital
and save him; those things aren't always fatal. Right again, but
he also could have jumped out the apartment window and suffered a certain death. He even might have obtained a gun in
some other way. Those who are intent on committing suicide
find a way to do so. The point is, the arguments, the "if only"
suppositions and the "yes, but" retorts, can go on forever.

BLAMING BEFORE THE FACT

Many suicide survivors were embarked on a guilt trip before the
suicide ever took place. Many people threaten suicide, either
verbally or by their actions, long before they take their own
lives. Many of you, having been faced with evidence of such suicidal ideas or impulses in your loved ones, took on a good deal
of responsibility for preventing the suicide. Very understandably,
you lived in terror of your loved one's taking her own life. Just
as understandably, though not as logically, you may have concluded that you would be responsible if she ever did kill herself.

Al is a good example. His mother was an alcoholic through
much of his growing-up years. On one occasion he witnessed
her menacing a relative with a knife. More often her destructive-
ness was directed at herself. One night she ran out of their
home and attempted to throw herself in front of a car. Like

many children of alcoholic parents (a category into which many suicide survivors fall), Al tried to look out for his mother. He took on the responsibility of stopping her from killing herself. For years, his biggest fear was that she would finally kill herself, and that he would be overwhelmed with guilt.

Al's story has a relatively happy ending. His mother did not kill herself. Even so, the memory of his dread of her possible suicide, and the terror he lived with for at least seven years, are among the most intense emotional experiences of his life.

An objective person hearing Al's story can empathize with his agony but can also recognize that he put this burden undeservedly on himself. Any objective observer can see that he was really powerless to control his mother's behavior. Nonetheless, many survivors take on this guilt.

THE ULTIMATE FORM OF BLACKMAIL

A threat of suicide is the ultimate form of emotional blackmail. It is used as a desperate attempt to control another's behavior. Many of you were explicitly threatened with suicide before the act was done. "I'll kill myself if you don't marry me!" or "I'll kill myself if you leave me!" are two of the most common forms that this threat can take. When such threats are made it is an indication that a real relationship is not viable. If you are threatened with suicide to make you commit to the relationship, you are in for endless trouble.

After you are involved in the relationship, when you have emotional bonds to the person, the dilemma is much more complicated. Now you can't walk away from the relationship without risking that which you fear most. What you should realize is that someone who can threaten you in this way is insensitive to you and your feelings. It may well be that he is too depressed or otherwise ill to be capable of sensitivity to you, but clearly he is not attending to your feelings and needs. He is no longer involved in a mutual, caring relationship with you.

We are talking a lot here about guilt that people may feel at the risk or threat of suicide, even when no suicide has taken place. It may be easier to see, in those cases, how it is grossly unfair and unreasonable for anyone to tell someone else that she will be responsible if he kills himself. Also, you are taking on a huge burden if you feel responsible for preventing another's suicide.

FOR A VERDICT OF "NOT GUILTY"

We could go on endlessly reciting specific "could've," "should've," and "would've" ruminations that we have heard from survivors in our support groups. There is really no point in doing so. The most fundamental statement we can make is: *You did not cause the suicide, and you are not responsible for it having happened!* The choice someone makes to commit suicide cannot be understood easily. It does not come to pass because of a single event or series of events. Perhaps you had separated from your husband before he committed suicide. Perhaps he even threatened to kill himself if you did not return to him. Did you cause his suicide? No! Hundreds of thousands of women separate from their husbands every year. Do all the husbands kill themselves? Of course not—only a minuscule fraction do.

Or perhaps you argued with your teenage daughter, placing some restriction on her before her suicide. Perhaps she even ran out of the room crying, "You're ruining my life. . . . I'm going to kill myself!" Did you cause her suicide? Again, *no!* Arguing with parents is a daily staple of teenage life. Most teenagers do not kill themselves when their parents do something they do not like.

All suicides have multiple causes. There is no one event, be it a divorce, rage at a parent, or learning that one has a fatal illness, that leads directly to suicide. Those who do choose to commit suicide after any of these events are driven by other forces as well. *You did not cause the suicide of your loved one because there is never just one cause for suicide!*

"The vast majority of those who request physician-assisted suicide or euthanasia are motivated primarily by dread of what will happen to them, rather than by their current pain or suffering."

EFFECTIVE PAIN MANAGEMENT CAN PREVENT ASSISTED SUICIDE

American Foundation for Suicide Prevention

The American Foundation for Suicide Prevention (AFSP), formerly known as the American Suicide Foundation, funds research, education, and treatment programs to prevent suicide. The following viewpoint is excerpted from AFSP's policy statement on physician-assisted suicide. The organization maintains that effective pain management can greatly reduce the number of terminally ill patients who request or desire death via assisted suicide. Most patients who become suicidal do not actually want to die, the organization asserts, but are merely trying to avoid the physical and mental suffering that their disease may cause.

As you read, consider the following questions:

1. How often is pain a factor in requests for assisted suicide or euthanasia, according to the American Foundation for Suicide Prevention?
2. In the organization's view, why do many doctors undertreat pain?
3. How does the legalization of physician-assisted suicide enhance a doctor's power, according to AFSP?

M ost people assume that seriously or terminally ill people who wish to end their lives are different than those who are otherwise suicidal. But an early reaction of many patients to the diagnosis of serious illness and possible death is terror, depression, and a wish to die. Such patients are not significantly different than patients who react to other crises in their lives with the desire to end the crisis by ending their lives.

ILLNESS, SUICIDE, AND ASSISTED SUICIDE

Physical illness influences the motivation for suicide; this was known long before today's movement to legalize assisting the suicide of patients who are seriously or terminally ill. Medical illness plays an important role in 25 percent of suicides, and this percentage rises with age, from 50 percent in suicides more than 50 years old, to over 70 percent in suicides older than 60.

Most suicide attempts reflect patients' ambivalence about dying, and those requesting assisted suicide show an equal ambivalence. If the doctor does not recognize that ambivalence, as well as the anxiety and depression that underlie the patient's request for death, the patient may become trapped by that request and die in a state of unrecognized terror.

The desire for death waxes and wanes in terminally ill patients, even among those few who articulate a persistent wish to die. When interviewed after two weeks, two-thirds of these patients show a significant decrease in the strengh of their desire to die. Some patients may voice suicidal thoughts in response to transient depression or severe pain, but these patients usually find relief with treatment of their depressive illness or pain, and thereafter they are grateful to be alive. Strikingly, the overwhelming majority of terminally ill patients fight for life to the end, only two to four percent of suicides occur in the context of terminal illness.

THE FEAR OF DEATH

Patients rarely cite the fear of death itself as their reason for requesting assisted suicide or euthanasia, but clinicians often see such patients transform their death-anxiety into fears about the circumstances of dying, fearing pain, dependency on others, loss of dignity, or the side effects of medical treatment. Focusing one's fear and rage on these palpable occurrences distracts patients from the fear of death itself.

For example, Tim was a professional in his early thirties when he developed acute myelocytic leukemia. He was told that medical treatment would give him a 25 percent chance of survival, and that without treatment he would die in a few months.

Tim, an ambitious executive whose focus on career success had led him to neglect his relationships with his wife and family, was stunned. His immediate reaction was a desperate, angry preoccupation with suicide and a request for support in carrying it out. He was worried about becoming dependent and feared both the symptoms of his disease and the side effects of treatment.

Once Tim could talk about the possibility or likelihood of his dying—what separation from his family and the destruction of his body meant to him—his desperation subsided. He accepted medical treatment and used the remaining months of his life to become closer to his wife and parents. At first he would not talk to his wife about his illness because of his resentment that she was going on with her life while he might not go on with his. A session with the two of them cleared the air and made it possible for them to talk openly with each other. Two days before he died, Tim talked about what he would have missed without the opportunity for a loving parting.

The last days of most patients' lives can be given such meaning if those treating them know how to engage them. Tim's need for communication with his wife, communication that was not possible until he voiced his envy and resentment over her going on with her life while he was probably not going to be doing so, finds parallels in the lives of most dying patients.

Like Tim, the vast majority of those who request physician-assisted suicide or euthanasia are motivated primarily by dread of what will happen to them rather than by their current pain or suffering. Patients do not know what to expect, and they cannot foresee how their conditions will unfold as they decline toward death. Facing this uncertainty, they fill the vacuum with their dreaded fantasies and fears. When a caring and knowledgeable physician addresses these fears, the request for an expedited death usually disappears. . . .

REASONS FOR REQUESTING DEATH

What of some of the reasons that patients give for requesting euthanasia—pain, loss of dignity, and the desire not to be dependent on others? All can contribute to depression and suffering that lead patients to want to die.

Pain is a factor in 30 percent of euthanasia requests, the major reason for the request in about 5 percent of cases. Pain can invariably be relieved if the physician is knowledgeable about how to do so. Unfortunately advances in our knowledge of how to treat pain have not been accompanied by adequate dissemination of that knowledge. Physicians undertreat even the most severe states of pain based on inappropriate fears of heavy sedation.

Most of the indignity of which patients justifiably complain is associated with futile medical treatments. Doctors are learning to forgo such treatment although patients are only beginning to learn that they can refuse them. On the other hand patients are also afraid of being abandoned by their doctors while they are dying. There is basis for these fears since only in the past decade have we begun to educate physicians that caring for patients they cannot cure is an integral part of medicine.

There are patients who find it hard to be dependent on others. Yet serious illness usually requires this. Dependency is hardest for patients when their families do not want that responsibility. A change in family attitudes, however, can modify the outcome in cases where patients wish to die. A 1989 Swedish study showed that when chronically ill patients attempted suicide, their overburdened families often did not want them resuscitated. But when social services stepped in and relieved the family's burden by sending in home care helpers, most patients wanted to live and their families wanted them to live, too.

LIFE-PROLONGING TECHNOLOGIES

Awareness of the dangers of physician-assisted suicide must be coupled with comparable awareness of the dangers of the unbridled use of life-prolonging medical technologies. It is now accepted practice—supported by the American Medical Association, the courts, and most churches—that patients need not be kept alive by invasive, artificial means, such as by feeding tubes.

With appropriate consent from the patient, family members, or other surrogate decision makers, it is considered the standard of medical care to forgo tube feeding while providing sufficient sedation to relieve any suffering. This is so even though the patient's death is the likely outcome. Patients must be made aware of this option. Doctors must learn when such an approach is appropriate. Hospitals must ensure that patients know that this kind of plan for care and sedation is available when it is appropriate and accepted.

What about a patient who is terminally ill but not in the last days of life, and requests euthanasia, saying he or she does not want to live with the physical and psychological distress of illness? Palliative care specialists and consultation-liaison psychiatrists in general hospitals see such patients frequently. When physicians respond to them empathetically, addressing their physical suffering, while making it possible for them to discuss their fears of death, most of these patients regain the desire to live.

What of those who say, "I don't want treatment even if it will make me feel better; I just want to die"? Should respect for their wishes require society to legalize assisted suicide and euthanasia? When so many patients will accept relief and will want to live if responded to sensitively by a caring and capable physician, when those who cannot be helped can be given sedation and allowed to die, we should not change social policy to accommodate those who are acutely suicidal and say "I want to die even if treatment will make me feel better.". . .

Our knowledge of how to minister to the needs of terminally ill people is one of medicine's finest achievements in the past decade, but disseminating that knowledge to the average physician has only begun. In the United States, doctors are not sufficiently trained in the relief of the pain and discomfort of terminally ill patients. Routine palliative care cannot be reserved for palliative care specialists; it must be the province of every physician.

Cancer pain has been most studied, and it is clear that most cancer pain can be relieved. Nevertheless, there are obstacles to patients' receiving this relief. Although close to 90 percent of physicians agree that it may be appropriate to use pain medication to relieve suffering even if it hastens a patient's death, fear of hastening death is a major reason physicians give inadequate doses of pain medication. The gap between what physicians know and what they do will be bridged only when every physician is expected to provide quality palliative care.

Medical school is the place to confront future physicians with the painful truth that they must develop skill to comfort and help those patients they cannot cure. Medical students can no longer be shielded from dying patients and told there is nothing to learn from them; on the contrary, students must be taught that comforting and caring for the dying is necessary to truly be a physician.

Physicians also need to involve patients more in the decisions about their treatment. All those who care for persons diagnosed with a terminal condition must communicate to those patients that at some point the best kind of medicine will likely involve shifting the goals of care from attempts at cure to active palliation. Patients also need to understand their right to refuse life-prolonging measures or other unwanted treatments, their right to forgo treatments before they have begun, and their right to terminate treatments that have commenced.

Furthermore, physicians must be encouraged to engage seriously ill patients and their families in a continuing realistic dialogue about the patient's changing condition, their mutually agreed upon goals of care, changes in these goals, palliative options, and clear accounts of what specific medical interventions can and cannot accomplish. This continuing conversation should not be deferred until the final phase of the illness. . . .

A REQUEST FOR RELIEF

Patients who request assisted suicide or euthanasia are usually asking in the strongest way they know for mental and physical relief from suffering. When that request is made to a caring, sensitive, and knowledgeable physician who can address their fear, relieve their suffering, and assure them that he or she will remain with them to the end, most patients no longer want to die and are grateful for the time remaining to them.

Patients making such a request are likely to benefit from talking to a psychiatrist about their desperation. Psychiatrists should not consent to the diminished role envisioned by euthanasia advocates of simply determining whether a patient is competent to make such a decision. It is the psychiatrist's broader traditional role that permits patients to openly air their fears, often making it possible for the psychiatrist to help relieve them.

What of the difficulties in finding caring and knowledgeable physicians willing and able to provide proper care during terminal illness? These problems are real, and have led some to advocate the legalization of assisted suicide and euthanasia, proposing that since we are not now providing sufficient numbers of patients with proper palliative care, we should make death a more accessible option.

Such a course amounts to meeting one social inequity with another—one that holds even greater adverse consequences. Wise social policy dictates that some people's wish for physician-assisted suicide cannot outweigh all other effects of its legalization on the many patients who would die inappropriately. To legalize assisted suicide and euthanasia would truly be what ethicist Daniel Callahan has called "self-determination run amok."

Clearly the wiser, more humane course is to successfully provide good palliative care to terminally ill patients. Advances in our knowledge of palliative care in the past twenty years make clear that care for the terminally ill does not require us to legalize assisted suicide and euthanasia. Our challenge, which can be met, is to bring that knowledge and that care to the critically ill.

Our success in providing palliative care for those who are terminally ill will not only address the suffering of the individual patients, but do much to preserve our social humanity. If we do not provide such care, legalization of assisted suicide and euthanasia will become the simplistic answer to the problem of dying. Euthanasia will become a way for all of us to ignore the genuine needs of terminally ill people.

If the advocates of legalization prevail, we will lose more lives to suicide (although we will call the deaths by a different name) than can be saved by the efforts of the American Foundation for Suicide Prevention and by all the other institutions working to prevent suicide in this country.

The tragic impact on depressed suicidal patients will be matched by what will happen to the elderly, the poor, and other terminally ill people. Assisted suicide and euthanasia will become routine ways of dealing with serious and terminal illness just as they have in the Netherlands; those without means will be under particular pressure to accept the euthanasia option. In the process, palliative care will be undercut for everyone.

Many people have the illusion that legalizing assisted suicide and euthanasia will give them greater autonomy. The Dutch experience teaches us that legalization of physician-assisted suicide enhances the power and control of doctors, not patients. In practice it is still the doctor who decides whether to perform euthanasia. He can suggest it, withhold obvious alternatives, ignore patients' ambivalence, and even put to death patients who have not requested it.

Euthanasia advocates have come to see suicide as a cure for disease and a way of appropriating death's power over the human capacity for control. In the process, they have derailed constructive efforts to better manage the final phase of life. Our social policy must be based on a larger and more positive concern for people who are terminally ill. It must reflect an expanded determination to relieve their physical pain, to discover the nature of their fears, and to diminish suffering by giving affirmation to the life that has been lived and still goes on.

"For [some] patients, [death] can . . .
be preferable to the side effects of the
treatments used to control pain."

EFFECTIVE PAIN MANAGEMENT MAY NOT PREVENT ASSISTED SUICIDE

Timothy E. Quill

In the following viewpoint, Timothy E. Quill maintains that
sometimes pain medications and other medical treatments are
unable to relieve the suffering of a terminally ill patient. In such
cases, he contends, assisted suicide may be the only option that
allows a patient a dignified death. Quill is a physician who has
written numerous articles supporting the right of terminally ill
patients to request assisted suicide. He is also the author of *Death
and Dignity: Making Choices and Taking Charge*, from which the following viewpoint is taken.

As you read, consider the following questions:

1. What is the "double effect," according to Quill?
2. Why do some caregivers feel abandoned by the medical
   profession, in the author's view?
3. What examples does Quill give of the distinction between a
   physician's taking an active or a passive role in helping a
   patient to die?

Comfort care, properly and comprehensively applied, can ensure a dignified death for most incurably ill patients. Unfortunately, there are anguishing exceptions where severe end-of-life suffering still occurs. The unrelieved suffering that stems from inadequate utilization of comfort care, or as the result of the restricted availability of medical care in general and of hospice programs in particular, is unnecessary and potentially reversible. These problems should be solved by educating doctors and by increasing the allocation of economic resources to health care for the under-served and to comfort care for the dying. Other limitations posed by the insoluble physical, emotional, and existential dilemmas incurably ill persons have to face are not so readily correctable. One of our most troubling challenges as physicians and caregivers is to respond to these patients for whom comprehensively applied comfort care is unable to adequately relieve their suffering, so that death seems the only sensible escape. . . .

Choosing Pain or Sedation

Most dying patients do not have a clearly defined route of exit. For those treated with comfort care, dying is usually at least tolerable, if not always peaceful. They may gradually slip into a coma, or develop a complication that precipitates a relatively benign final phase that is effectively managed using comfort-care principles. For others, death does not come easily in spite of a comfort-oriented approach. Some patients are forced to live on the edge of death for weeks or even months in semi-conscious states. They receive enough medication to keep them from being aware of their pain, but not so much that the medication will precipitate their death. Such patients must often make very difficult choices on a daily basis between pain and sedation. If feeding tubes or intravenous fluids are part of the treatment plan, patients can remain in this twilight zone indefinitely—a state where they are in too much pain to be awake, but have no immediate problem to precipitate death. For some people, such prolongation of dying might have a purpose; for others, it is meaningless and even cruel.

For a few patients, even those on hospice programs, the end can be agonizing and completely out of their control. Some have progressive, untreatable medical problems that defy solution throughout the final course of their illness. Others are able to be maintained with relative comfort and dignity through most of their terminal illness, but the illness accelerates in its maliciousness toward the end. Some patients infected with human immunodeficiency virus (HIV) experience such ends. Not infrequently, near the end of a long and heroic struggle against the disease and its associated infections, the process begins irreversibly to attack their brain and eyesight. Many HIV-infected patients have become experts on their disease, both through extensive reading and through the experience of caring for others infected with the virus. For those who place extreme value on their physical and intellectual integrity, living out their final time with the progressive dementia associated with HIV can be far worse than death. "What dignity can be found dying demented, lying in my own feces, unaware of my surroundings?" they ask. The promise of comfort care is not overly soothing to some who have seen and may personally face this tragic end. A few choose an active end to their struggle through suicide, often acting in secret, isolated from their health-care providers and friends. Forcing such patients to choose between a "natural" death that they would find humiliating and secretly bypassing this end through suicide cannot be a part of humane care. The notion that such patients have to face this agonizing decision alone, often in secrecy, violates basic principles of humane care.

It is not only patients with HIV who force us to face the limits of a comfort-oriented approach. Another dramatic, at times excruciating lesson comes from the patients with lung or oral cancer who are dying of respiratory failure. These patients struggle to breathe, and are often continuously coughing and producing mucous in copious amounts. The morphine which we use to treat their pain and ease their struggle is helpful, though at times it may indirectly lessen the drive to breathe and therefore inadvertently hasten death. This is a classic example of the "double effect," and is completely acceptable under principles of comfort care. When such patients eventually slip painlessly into a coma and die without an overwhelming struggle, we feel good about our job and about the efficacy of comfort care.

However, some patients with incurable respiratory problems have the opposite experience—they endure a panicked, suffocating struggle just prior to death that is very much like drowning. Dying of suffocation can be an excruciating ordeal for both the patient and the caregivers. The double effect suggests that one should give enough pain medicine to relieve suffering, but not an amount that intentionally precipitates death. Therefore, these agonizing ends are sometimes prolonged because of the unacceptability of directly intending death, even if death is the only escape from suffering. Some patients can live in an agonizing twilight between suffocation and death because of the ambiguity of our intentions. Attending doctors are only rarely at the bedside for these occurrences. More often it is nurses or family members who are operating under unclear directives with double meanings like "Keep him comfortable," or, "You can give her a little extra if she seems to need it." I am certain that some health-care providers and family members give patients enough medication to help their patient die under such circumstances, because most caring persons cannot continue to be present and watch such agony without responding.

ABANDONED BY THE MEDICAL PROFESSION

The letters I have received [from supporters of assisted suicide] suggest that caregivers at the bedside feel abandoned by the medical profession under these circumstances. The profession appears to turn its back in these horrible moments in order to keep its intentions pure. Doctors cannot intentionally facilitate death, even if death is the only way to relieve a patient's overwhelming suffering. By maintaining this artificial distinction, our profession undermines the true intent of comfort care: to help people maintain dignity, control, and comfort all the way through the final phase of their illness until death. Because so many family members and friends have witnessed such very troubling deaths, it appears that this experience also undermines the public's trust that doctors will not abandon them if they are unfortunate enough to experience unbearable suffering prior to death.

The double effect captures a paradox in the care of the dying. It allows one to treat suffering with powerful measures that may hasten death. But intentionally accelerating death, even if it is the only escape from intolerable suffering, is not acceptable. The double effect does not acknowledge the fact that, for some patients, death is preferable to unremitting suffering. For other patients, it can also be preferable to the side effects of the treatments used to control pain and other symptoms. There is nothing selfish or improper about wanting a dignified, controlled death if one is incurably ill and has no other sensible options.

Many medical ethicists make a clear distinction between an active and passive role on the part of the physician in helping a patient to die. It is acceptable, for example, for a doctor to help a patient die by stopping a life-sustaining treatment, when requested to do so by the patient or if the treatment becomes medically futile. But it is not acceptable for a doctor actively to help a patient die who has an equal or greater amount of suffering, but who is not dependent on life-sustaining treatment that can be discontinued. Mr. P., a man with a brain tumor, was living a life without personal meaning, intolerable by almost anyone's standards, and surely by his own. Once we realized that one of his treatments was life-sustaining, we were able to offer him the option of stopping it with the purpose of "relieving his suffering." We knew that only death would provide this relief, but we could not outwardly show intent to produce death. Had Mr. P. not been on steroids, or had we not realized that they could be stopped, then he would have been forced to continue to live against his own wishes, with no hope of an exit other than a "natural" death under the current limitations of comfort care. Those who are dependent on life-sustaining treatments are the only patients who receive the medical right to choose death. No matter how excruciating and unrelenting their suffering, or how persuasive and rational their request, other patients are not allowed this possibility within current constraints. Patients who have the courage, physical strength, and means to act alone can still release themselves through suicide; but most are trapped to live out their sentence until death comes more passively and, at times, more agonizingly.

Patients who have kidney failure and are dependent on dialysis treatment are also given the option of choosing death. Dialysis is an example of a life-sustaining medical intervention with

---

PHYSICAL PAIN IS NOT THE CAUSE

The wish for death by assisted suicide in a person suffering from AIDS or the early stages of Alzheimer's disease is related to the degradations and anxieties attendant to physical pain, rather than to just the physical pain itself, which can be controlled by appropriate doses of medicine. . . .

Physical pain . . . is not the kind of pain that is implicated in most suicide. Which leads us now to the kind of pain that is involved—namely, psychological pain, or psychache. . . .

Psychache is the hurt, anguish, or ache that takes hold in the mind. It is intrinsically psychological—the pain of excessively felt shame, guilt, fear, anxiety, loneliness, angst, dread of growing old or of dying badly. When psychache occurs, its introspective reality is undeniable. Suicide happens when the psychache is deemed unbearable and death is actively sought to stop the unceasing flow of painful consciousness. Suicide is a tragic drama in the mind.

What my research has taught me is that only a small minority of cases of excessive psychological pain result in suicide, but every case of suicide stems from excessive psychache.

Edwin S. Shneidman, *The Suicidal Mind*, 1996.

---

extraordinary benefits and substantial burdens. It can prolong the life of a patient whose kidneys have failed while they await a donor for potential transplantation. Others who are not candidates for transplantation can be maintained indefinitely with three half days of dialysis each week. The treatments are time-consuming and have significant burdens in terms of repeated needle sticks, periods of nausea and weakness, and a host of potential physical, social, and financial complications. For most people, however, the burdens of dialysis, though considerable, are outweighed by the benefit of continued life.

THE ONLY GOOD OPTION

Yet some patients on dialysis reach a point where the requirements of the treatment, combined with the suffering and limitations associated with their underlying illnesses, outweigh any meaning or enjoyment they can get out of life. It is generally accepted that the decision to discontinue dialysis can be rational—that a dialysis patient can reach a point where death is preferable to continued life with the accompanying burdens of treatment and illness. All attempts should be made to ensure that the patient's request to discontinue dialysis is not distorted by a treatable depression, or by unaddressed problems such as chronic pain. Despite these qualifications, many patients on dialysis die from having voluntarily discontinued treatment. The doctor plays an active role in ensuring that the patient has explored all other options, knows the consequences of his or her decision, and is not suffering from a distorting, treatable mental or physical illness. Yet, ethically, the doctor's role is passive in terms of helping the patient to die, since it is the patient who is discontinuing a life-sustaining treatment. In allowing the patient to stop dialysis, doctor and patient have come to acknowledge that there are no good options other than death. For the few days between the time dialysis is stopped and the patient dies, the patient is treated using comfort-care principles. The time frame is short, and patients can be heavily sedated in the interest of comfort while they await death.

In cases where the patient is dependent on a life-sustaining treatment, a doctor can ethically and legally assist the patient to achieve a relatively rapid, humane death. But there are frightening examples of the absurd lengths to which caring medical professionals must go to avoid directly assisting patients to die who are not dependent on such measures, in order to keep their intentions "pure." The following story was told to me informally by a colleague:

Mrs. B.

Mrs. B. had had breast cancer for over ten years. For the first five years of her illness she lived fully, continuing her job as a schoolteacher, being minimally bothered by her disease. But she unfortunately had an aggressive form of breast cancer, and the last five years of her life were mired by repeated hospitalizations, surgeries, hormonal therapies, chemotherapy and radiation. At age sixty, she was nearing the end of a long ordeal—exhausted, weary, and losing hope of finding any solution that would have meaning for her. Her illness had forced her to give up teaching prematurely, and she was becoming more and more dependent on her three children and the health care system. She had found the last six months completely empty, since she was bedbound from repeated fractures and forced to move to a nursing facility that also served as a hospice. There she made a few new friends and had some moments with her family that she viewed as tolerable. Yet, as she became weaker and could no longer read or even care for her basic bodily functions, she found her continued existence unbearable.

Mrs. B. clearly wanted to die. Her life had been stripped of all that was important to her. Death was the only thing she looked forward to. She no longer feared death, but was terrified about continuing to live under the current circumstances. She had nothing left to give.

As occurs all too often, death did not come in a timely way. Feeling trapped and desperate, Mrs. B. asked her personal physician for help. Her doctor cared deeply about Mrs. B. She knew from their shared, grueling experience, and from in-depth exploration of her reasoning, that Mrs. B.'s request was rational, and not distorted by depression. The doctor wanted to be helpful, but feared the potential professional and legal effects of providing active assistance. After getting permission from Mrs. B., the doctor decided to present the dilemma to the hospital ethics committee for guidance.

I am not privy to the deliberations of the ethics committee, but I do know their recommendations. They suggested that the physician could actively treat Mrs. B.'s suffering by giving her enough morphine and sedation so that she became unconscious (therefore unaware of her suffering) and then letting her die by dehydration. This method, they felt, would be within the acceptable limits of comfort care, using the double effect to treat her suffering aggressively without intending death. Death would come passively, they presumably reasoned, through a more "natural" process. The committee suggested that providing active assistance by more forthrightly helping the patient to die would be outside of current professional and legal restraints, and therefore unadvisable.

The doctor was very ambivalent and somewhat disturbed by the plan, but she reported the option to Mrs. B., who knew of the consultation. The doctor felt it was the only way she could respond to Mrs. B.'s request without taking a very large personal risk. (In fact, the risk of providing more "active" assistance had become even greater now that the patient's dilemma had been discussed in a relatively public forum.) Mrs. B. accepted the only option she had that would eventually ensure death. She subsequently said goodbye to her family and closest friends, and was put on an intravenous drip that contained morphine and a sedative, until she was unarousable. She remained in this state for ten days before dying, periodically attended by friends and family who found the experience deeply disturbing. Mrs. B.'s family had accepted her wish to die, but forcing her into a medically induced twilight zone so that she could then die of "natural causes" seemed macabre.

Mrs. B. was the second patient I heard of who was subjected to such a procedure. The solution seems humane on the surface, but feels more cruel and absurd as one thinks deeply about it. What was the intention of the treatment, or the committee, for that matter? What is our professional responsibility when death is clearly preferable to continued living and earnestly desired by the patient? If death is the only way the patient has to relieve suffering, then should it not be provided in the most humane manner possible when requested?

Many of the letters I received commented that we treat our pets better than we treat ourselves and our families. We would never allow our pets to be put into a coma so they could die of dehydration over a ten-day period, particularly if they could tell us that they were ready to die. It would be cruel to torture them prior to death. We love them too much to allow this to happen. Yet for human beings who have clearly articulated their wishes, our hands are tied—tied in part because we have difficulty accepting that for humans, death is sometimes the only escape from intolerable suffering. Allowing someone a peaceful, dignified death under such terrible circumstances can be a very sad, loving gift. Provided that all other options have been thoroughly explored and understood, and we are certain that this is what the patient wants, it may be the best of a very limited number of options one can offer under such dire circumstances.

> "Schools could help children develop traits, habits, and skills that would make it less likely that they would ever become suicidal."

Schools Can Help Prevent Suicide

David Lester

In the following viewpoint, David Lester asserts that teachers and counselors can prevent student suicide by identifying and aiding students who are suicidal. Schools can also help prevent suicide by improving student self-esteem and by providing crisis counseling, Lester argues. However, he maintains, suicide awareness programs for students are not always highly effective and should be carefully evaluated before being implemented. Lester is a professor of psychology at Richard Stockton State College in New Jersey and the author of *The Cruelest Death: The Enigma of Adolescent Suicide*, from which this viewpoint is taken.

As you read, consider the following questions:
1. What are five reasons why schools should be involved in suicide prevention, according to J. Smith, as cited by Lester?
2. What is primary prevention, according to Lester?
3. What are four criticisms of the use of suicide prevention programs in schools, according to Lester?

Reprinted, with permission, from David Lester, *The Cruelest Death: The Enigma of Adolescent Suicide* (Philadelphia: The Charles Press, Publishers, 1993). References in the original have been omitted in some cases in this reprint. Please consult the original book for further information.

Beginning in the 1980s, elementary schools became more involved in suicide prevention. Students are in school five days a week, for seven or eight hours a day, for nine months each year. Peers, teachers and school counselors are constantly in close contact with students and are, therefore, in an ideal position to notice signs of an impending suicidal crisis and to intervene to prevent it from happening.

WHY SCHOOLS SHOULD BE INVOLVED

Does this close proximity of students to teachers mean that educational institutions should necessarily be involved in suicide prevention? J. Smith has suggested issues that he believes provide reasons why schools should be involved. First, schools now do a good deal more than teach students academics; they have added to their pursuits the goals of helping students develop into mature and productive citizens, and this typically includes developing psychological and psychiatric health.

Second, schools try to resolve other problems that interfere with education, such as learning disabilities and obvious psychiatric problems; suicide is certainly a problem that interferes with education. Third, schools have developed resources such as counseling services that are useful for suicide prevention. Fourth, suicide prevention in the schools typically includes an educational component, and so suicide prevention fits in well with the school's health program.

Finally, perhaps the most forceful argument of all, schools have begun to lose the lawsuits that have been brought against them by parents of students who committed suicide. Often, parents feel that if their child has been displaying suicidal behavior at school, then the school should have some responsibility for intervening.

Thus far, there have been three major issues that have emerged in efforts to bring suicide prevention to schools: staff training in suicide prevention, student education in suicide prevention, and the establishment of guidelines and procedures for dealing with the aftermath of a suicide of a student in the school.

SUICIDE AWARENESS TRAINING

Many programs have been established to increase suicide awareness in educators, parents and students. D. Ryerson, for example, has set up several programs: a 3-hour intensive seminar for educators that covers facts about suicide and techniques of crisis intervention; less intensive programs that cover the same issues for parents; and 4- to 6-hour workshops that provide information on suicide and its prevention for students. The programs also increase awareness of community resources so that students in crisis can be referred for appropriate help.

Aldo Spirito and co-workers trained teachers to provide a 6-week curriculum for students in health classes. The content of the course focused on knowledge, attitudes and behaviors related to suicide, with special attention given to destroying the myths about suicide (such as "Those who talk about it won't do it"). Risk factors and warning signs were reviewed, and students were helped to feel compassion rather than hostility for those in a suicidal crisis. Students were also trained to respond to suicidal peers by using the techniques of active listening (also known as person-centered counseling), providing social support, and trying to get the student to seek help.

PRIMARY PREVENTION

Another area in which schools can work well with students, an area that has been neglected by psychologists and psychiatrists, is primary prevention—in other words, preventing the problem before it starts. Suicide prevention, on the other hand, is based on devising ways of intervening once an individual is in a suicidal crisis. It has been hard to devise strategies to prevent people from becoming suicidal.

Schools provide an excellent opportunity for primary prevention. Schools could help children develop traits, habits, and skills that would make it less likely that they would ever become suicidal.

To date, school programs have focused primarily on improving the self-esteem of young children, beginning as early as kindergarten. Goals have been established (such as providing children with opportunities for experiencing success and independence), and curricula have been devised.

POSTVENTION IN SCHOOLS

Our schools need to establish guidelines for teachers on how to deal with students when there is a crisis. Guidelines can facilitate coping with any kind of crisis. Recently, one school experienced the crash of a plane with a helicopter over a playground where many young students were playing. As a result several children were killed and others received severe burns. Mass murders have occurred on school grounds, school buses have crashed causing loss of life, and the disaster of the space shuttle *Challenger* had traumatic consequences for the school staff and children whose teacher was on board. Though perhaps less dramatic, the suicide of a student can also cause a severe crisis for the school, including emotional upset in many of the students, and this can even precipitate more suicides.

Since community resources are usually required for good postvention, it is necessary to contact community resources before any trauma occurs so that coordination and networking arrangements can be worked out. Key agencies must be brought in and community leaders must be involved.

AN IMPORTANT BENEFIT

The most important benefit [of suicide prevention counselors in schools] is that the suicidal student will have an advocate readily available eight hours a day who will be knowledgeable about the thoughts and feelings the student is experiencing, able to interpret the individuals' behavior towards others more effectively, and will accomplish these tasks in an empathetic fashion to the student. It is estimated between 3–6 percent of all high school students require the direct services of a suicide prevention team. Not only at-risk students, but all students, teachers, and members of the community benefit from the diverse activities of this team.

Barry D. Garfinkel, *Report of the Secretary's Task Force on Youth Suicide*, 1989.

Administrators should have guidelines established for dealing with the news media, especially since the news media can exacerbate a crisis by the way in which they report it. The Centers for Disease Control have even expressed concern over this issue and have published a set of guidelines. Administrators should also have plans for dealing with distraught parents. An obvious first step would be to designate specific staff members for these tasks.

It would be useful for schools to have staff that are already trained to deal with crises and they should make previous arrangements with local mental health facilities who are willing to provide counselors and consultants for times of crisis, for some students (and staff) may require immediate crisis intervention.

Teachers (and other staff, even including the school bus drivers) should be trained to recognize when a student seems to be in distress. For some students, the distress may not occur immediately after the trauma, but rather it may develop over the next few days or weeks as reality sinks in. Thus, a continuing program lasting several months is important, though of course the level of effort involved should decline over time. A good set of guidelines for postvention in schools has been provided by Susanne Wenckstern and Antoon Leenaars.

The establishment of procedures for dealing with trauma in a school and the introduction of curricula designed to improve the psychological health of children and adolescents cannot be faulted. There has, however, been some criticism of programs to educate students about suicide and suicide prevention. Alan L. Berman noted that schools in the United States apparently cannot teach the basic skills of reading, writing and arithmetic very well. How can they be expected to divert resources to teach students about suicide in addition to all of the other social issues that parents demand that schools focus on (such as AIDS, drug abuse and sexual behavior)? The result is that suicide awareness programs are brief one-time workshops, and there is no reason to believe that such brief programs will be effective.

Suicide awareness programs are frequently not evaluated and, when they are, they occasionally (but not always) reveal disturbing conclusions. David Shaffer and co-workers found that the programs they evaluated did not change student attitudes toward the management of suicide, or whether the students would seek counseling if they were in crisis. A small, but significant, percentage of the students at high risk for suicide (for example, those who had attempted suicide in the past) reported that the program had actually increased the difficulties they had in dealing with their problems.

There is a danger too in romanticizing suicide as a possible solution to life's difficulties. For comparison, consider AIDS. Contracting AIDS would not seem to be an attractive goal for anyone. It can be a very dangerous side effect of pleasure-seeking behavior. It should, therefore, be relatively easy to educate people on how to avoid catching it, but this has proven quite difficult.

In contrast, for those depressed and in crisis, suicide seems to be a viable, even a good choice. Talking about suicide may decrease the fear of death by providing intellectual control over such emotions. Describing cases of suicide, especially those portrayed in videos and television specials for students, may provide role models with whom the suicidal student can identify.

MORE EVALUATION IS NEEDED

In conclusion, while primary prevention of suicide (and other psychological problems) in schoolchildren seems to be an excellent idea and while all schools should have established procedures for dealing with crises, the design and provision of suicide awareness programs, particularly those for the students, requires a great deal more thought and evaluation before we can be comfortable with them.

"If we are to significantly reduce the incidence of assisted suicide . . . among older women in America, we must . . . change our attitudes about older women."

CHANGING SOCIETY'S ATTITUDE TOWARD THE ELDERLY CAN HELP PREVENT SUICIDE

Nancy J. Osgood and Susan A. Eisenhandler

Society's negative attitudes toward women and the elderly give many older women a feeling of worthlessness, assert Nancy J. Osgood and Susan A. Eisenhandler. The authors contend in the following viewpoint that older women in American society are adversely affected by sexist and ageist stereotypes, so it is not surprising that they compose the majority of assisted suicide victims. Society must change its attitude toward and treatment of older women to reduce the number of elderly women suicide victims, they maintain. Osgood is a professor of gerontology and sociology at the Virginia Commonwealth University/Medical College of Virginia in Richmond. Eisenhandler is an assistant professor of sociology at the University of Connecticut in Storrs.

As you read, consider the following questions:

1. What percentage of euthanasia victims between 1980 and 1985 were over the age of sixty, according to Derek Humphry and Ann Wickett, as cited by the authors?
2. How does living in a nursing home contribute to acquiescent suicide, in the authors' opinion?
3. What factors contributed to Irene's depression and suicidal tendencies, according to Osgood and Eisenhandler?

From Nancy J. Osgood and Susan A. Eisenhandler, "Gender and Assisted and Acquiescent Suicide: A Suicidologist's Perspective," *Issues in Law and Medicine*, Spring 1994. Reprinted with permission. References in the original have been omitted here.

Pope John Paul II predicted that the great moral issue of the 1980s would be euthanasia. His prediction has indeed proven to be correct. According to Derek Humphry and Ann Wickett, of all euthanasia cases reported between 1920 and 1985, seventy percent occurred during the last five years of this period. Not surprisingly, the majority of people involved in these euthanasia cases were old. Sixty-four percent were over the age of sixty, while fifty-one percent were over seventy.

Unlike euthanasia, in which consent of the victim is not necessary, assisted suicide implies the consent of and, in many cases, the request of the victim. The great moral issue of the 1990s is the issue of assisted suicide.

JANET ADKINS AND DR. KEVORKIAN

According to Nancy J. Osgood in *Suicide in Later Life: Recognizing the Warning Signs*, Dr. Jack Kevorkian brought the issue to the fore when he participated in the suicide of Janet Adkins:

> On June 4, 1990, 54-year-old Janet Adkins ended her life lying on a cot in the back of a Volkswagen van parked in a Michigan suburb. Aided by a retired pathologist, Dr. Jack Kevorkian, Adkins was hooked up to his homemade "suicide machine." She had a needle inserted in her arm, which first started saline flowing and, then when she pressed the button on the macabre death machine, sent first a sedative and then deadly potassium chloride flowing into her veins. . . .

Since Dr. Kevorkian assisted Janet Adkins in 1990 with ending her life, he has assisted in the suicides of several more people. The majority of his "victims" have been middle-aged women. If the Kevorkian cases accurately reflect the total of all assisted suicide cases, then it would appear that individuals who die from assisted suicide are more likely to be older women. . . .

AGE AND GENDER ISSUES

These cases have brought dramatically to the nation's attention the debate over the right to die with dignity and the ethics of helping others to commit suicide. Suicide and assisted suicide are issues particularly relevant to older members of our society. Dramatic medical advances have greatly increased life expectancy but also have increased the period of chronic illness and disability. A growing population of older citizens places considerably greater financial and social demands on society. The rapid rate of cultural change, resulting in a situation in which older people may have outlived their previous roles and sources of value and meaning, has spawned moral and ethical dilemmas about suicide and assisted suicide among older persons.

The majority of victims of assisted suicide in this country are women. Compared to men, women are also much more likely to be the victims in murder/suicides, in which the man kills his wife and then himself. When a love pact suicide is committed and husband and wife commit suicide together, women who die with their spouses often are not as physically sick or mentally impaired as the man, but they still die with him. In 1983 Cynthia Koestler, only fifty-five years old and in perfect health, chose to die with her husband, author Arthur Koestler, age seventy-seven, who was suffering from Parkinson's disease. According to close friends of the Koestlers and the writings of Cynthia herself, Cynthia felt that she could not live without Arthur. Apparently Cynthia's personal identity and life were so bound up in her famous husband that, when he chose to die, she automatically chose to die with him.

AGE OF EUTHANASIA PATIENTS 1980–1985

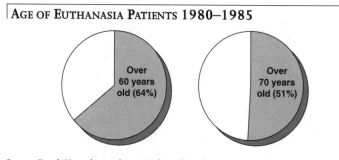

Over 60 years old (64%)

Over 70 years old (51%)

Source: Derek Humphry and Ann Wickett, *The Right to Die: Understanding Euthanasia*, 1987.

Because the majority of victims of assisted suicide are women, issues of gender are paramount. Compared to men in American society, women are socially and economically disadvantaged. They are much less likely than men to hold positions of status and authority. They are much more likely than men to be powerless. The stereotypical view of women views them as dependent, passive, weak, and hysterical. According to Silvia S. Canetto, "The idea that women *succumb* to love, suicide, and suicide for love has a long tradition in Western culture."

Negative myths and stereotypes about older women abound in our culture. Older women are viewed as "old hags" and "old bags," frumpy, ditzy, and meddlesome. Sarah Matthews, who interviewed older women in their seventies, found that they were ashamed of their age. Ageism and sexism force many older women to experience self-derogation and to feel dejected, degraded, devalued, useless, and worthless.

In view of the sexism and ageism experienced by older women in our society, it is not surprising that older women are so often the victims of assisted suicide. Confronted with physical health problems or serious mental decline and the prospect that they will unduly burden their family and their society, these women make the ultimate sacrifice and choose to end their lives. Requesting assistance to die to avoid burdening those she loves, or choosing to die with the man she loves, even if she is healthy and mentally alert, represent desperate acts of a powerless person. Older women who receive assistance in dying are usually assisted by their husbands or physicians, who are generally men. . . .

ACQUIESCENT SUICIDE

A less visible, less dramatic, but no less real problem is what might be called acquiescent suicide. Bound as it is in the discourse of academic disciplines and legal definitions of accountability, the controversy over assisted suicide misses the subtle and perhaps more widespread phenomenon of people who turn away from life in relatively quiet and unnoticed ways. Current discussions of assisted suicide are notable because in large part they overlook the more subtle and almost certainly more widespread phenomenon of individuals, particularly older adults, who acquiesce to serious illness (decline food and treatment, become uninterested in maintaining desired social relationships) and in so doing end their own lives quietly and slowly without the active assistance of others. This form of suicide may characterize the experience of powerless groups, older women among them, whose daily lives and orientation to time are structured by institutional settings and the adults who staff these settings.

In this viewpoint we define acquiescent suicide and present a case study of an older woman who lived in a long-term care facility and who took her own life. Through a qualitative analysis of case study materials, we argue that this woman's death illustrates a form of suicide that emerges when women are absorbed by a physical and social context that simultaneously diminishes their worth and will not brook their release. Unlike the traditional dichotomy of passive versus active suicide, or the more current dichotomy of self-initiated versus assisted suicide, the phrase *acquiescent suicide* represents a form of suicide that occurs in relatively isolated settings with hierarchical patterns of interaction that intensify the powerlessness perceived and felt by residents. The process of institutionalization that puts people aside for some reasonable purpose—e.g., treatment or care—cloaks and influences patterns of resignation and self-destruction that are all the more disquieting to think about because they are, in contrast to other forms of suicide, so quiet, subtle, and likely to be overlooked. Our analysis reveals that a particular kind of social world creates a milieu that has a profound influence upon older women and may, for some women, stimulate their quiet, sometimes unnoticed efforts to end their own lives. . . .

Nursing home residency exposes older adults to the depersonalization and control that challenges the strongest individual identities and vitiates the identities of those with more tenuous social and psychological anchors of self and identity. Within the ecological context of the nursing home, this means that many older adults are only capable of engaging in two "lines of adaptation"—withdrawal and intransigence.

A HEIGHTENED SENSITIVITY

The dynamics of gender, combined with the social history or biography that leads to nursing home residence, make it likely that older women have heightened sensitivity to the social context that now is the stage for their lives and for their deaths. The silent struggle against confinement—rejecting medication, refusing food and interaction—mounted by older women in nursing homes becomes their means of release from the environment. By their own hand, some women acquiesce to the institutional context and commit suicide, a gradual but no less certain death than the suicides that involve other methods. Many adults do not, and in terms of health cannot, sustain the balance between separateness and integration of adult identity, or personality, in the total institution of a nursing home. Instead, many yield to the social context. When individuals yield identity, acquiescent suicide is a possible outcome. Findings from a large-scale national study of suicide in long-term care facilities reveal that many older residents in long-term care institutions engage in suicidal acts. . . .

DEVASTATION AND DESPAIR

The contextual dynamics of institutional living are complicated, particularly when the individuals and groups institutionalized are socially marginal on a host of dimensions—age, gender, health status, and mobility—as is the older woman we will describe in the next part of this viewpoint. When groups and individuals are confined to an institution, their entire range of action and interaction is restricted. When extremely devalued individuals, usually in fair to poor physical health, are placed in nursing homes, the loss of control, freedom, and power can be magnified, and life is experienced as devastating. All the more devastating is the reality that this home is the last home: there will be no other human setting. Experienced in this way, life becomes a form of imprisonment accompanied by great despair. Without sustained social support from at least one other person, the individual gradually accommodates or moves toward becoming one with the social ecology surrounding the self.

SOCIETY'S NEGATIVE ATTITUDES

Much has been written about the negative attitudes, or ageism, toward aging and the elderly, that exist in subtle and more obvious ways in our society. The old tend to be viewed as expendable, as having lived long enough and, perhaps, as having outlived their usefulness. Daily, the high value of youth and the devaluing of old age are apparent in advertisements, television, and other media. . . .

Attitudinal research suggests that people regard suicide as more acceptable when the person's precipitating illness is cancer and when the person committing suicide is elderly. These attitudes are complex and will require further study as well as educational efforts to combat myths and negative attitudes toward the old and old age as the debate over these issues continue. . . .

Death by one's own hand is premature at *any* age and the premature deaths of older adults constitute a loss of talent and resources that no society can accept. We must improve and increase our efforts to prevent and reduce such avoidable tragedies and enhance the lives of elders.

John L. McIntosh, *Suicide and Life-Threatening Behavior*, Spring 1995.

In this manner, suicide is a kind of acquiescence to social context. As we will see, suicidal older women turn into the context as a way of getting out of the context. That is to say, they obliterate the self by turning away the food, medicines, and social relationships that would keep them alive. To say such suicides are passive misses the analytical point that the context itself overwhelms some individuals and dismisses the dynamics of gender inequity that shape the context itself. Indeed, a focus on the method or style of suicide may provide spurious specification of the problem, directing attention and intervention to establishing food, medication, and other behavioral directives and procedures that do very little to make the nursing home a better place to live. . . .

IRENE: A CASE OF ACQUIESCENT SUICIDE

We now take up the case of Irene described by Nancy J. Osgood et al. in *Suicide Among the Elderly in Long-Term Care Facilities*:

> Irene was a person of exceptional beauty. When introduced, she was dressed in a pair of tight-fitting black slacks, which enhanced her shapely figure, and a bright purple silk blouse, a birthday gift from her friends. Her snow-white hair was perfectly in place, and her make-up impeccable. She had just returned to the facility from an evening out with some younger friends. The smile on her face and the sparkle in her eyes reflected the excitement of a teenager returning from a date. She was open and charming, an unforgettable individual. Because of her youthful 50's presence, one could barely believe that Irene, a widow, was 81 years of age, and had raised 11 children on a farm outside the city. She had lived in the nursing home approximately one week and went there at the insistence of the family.
>
> The last time the interviewer saw Irene alive, just two months after their initial meeting, she was barely recognizable. Her appearance was disheveled, her face pale and sunken, and, her lips a bluish color, she rapidly paced back and forth near the pay phone. A healing laceration was observed over her left eye. . . .
>
> Notations in the medical record and interviews with staff members revealed that Irene was a very lonely and depressed person, and at one point had attempted to end her own life by refusing to eat, drink, or take medication. Frequent expressions of loneliness, feelings of family rejection and abandonment, and periods of crying were also noted. A more in-depth examination of the medical record, interviews with staff, and with Irene uncovered pertinent factors which contributed to depression and suicidal behavior. Chief among these was family rejection. Irene had spent her entire life caring for her children. She had given up the dream of teaching school in deference to devoted motherhood. Times had been very difficult for Irene and her family. A hard worker, she scrubbed other people's homes, took in laundry and sewing, made clothes for the children from the discards of others, and helped her husband farm their land, often working from dawn to dusk, to help make ends meet.
>
> A few of Irene's children completed college on their own, all married well and were financially independent. She was proud of her oldest son, a professor in a local university. Neither the children nor the grandchildren visited Irene very often during her residency in the nursing home. Ironically, one of her granddaughters was employed by the facility, but seldom visited her grandmother. Irene felt totally rejected and abandoned by the children she devoted her life to. "I just want to be wanted. When you get

old, your family just forgets you and you have no purpose in life anymore. Eleven children and no place to go in the end."

Another major factor contributing to Irene's depression and suicidal ruminations was her financial situation. The loss of the family farm was the most devastating loss she and her husband had suffered. Financial loss was severe and they never recovered. She was destitute after her husband's death, and ashamed and embarrassed that she was forced to live on welfare to meet expenditures. Because she was unable to afford many new clothes, she made do and ate little to avoid a weight gain. As a Medicaid resident in the nursing home, she received less than $35 a month for necessary expenditures, and had little left over for extras. Unless her friends treated her to a night out, she could not afford that luxury she so enjoyed. . . .

Reduced to dependent status in the nursing home, with many rules and regulations, she could not adjust to the loss of independence, freedom, and personal autonomy. She viewed herself as trapped, and likened her feelings to those of a caged animal, stating, "If they make me stay here, then my life is over. I might just as well be dead.". . .

Just a Shadow

In two months, Irene was literally a shadow of the woman she had been when she entered the nursing home. The unresolved shame and anxiety Irene felt about her financial ruin and her disappointment about the kind of care provided by her eleven children dashed expectations about the future and voided the meaning of her life.

After her move into the home, Irene drew upon her present circumstance and past life to construct a future that was nihilistic. This future void, combined with a present crisis of spirit and the imminence of bodily death, made life in the restrictive setting of a home untenable. Unfortunately, to use a phrase from a Dylan Thomas poem, going "gentle into that good night" seemed necessary and desirable to Irene.

Irene's case is not atypical. Many older women in nursing homes and other long-term care institutions across the country acquiesce to the social context in which they find themselves living and dying. The case of Irene is not offered as an indictment of a particular nursing home or of nursing homes in general. Women like Irene are also found living in their own homes in the community. However, the institutional setting by its very nature is a social and ecological environment that is particularly conducive to acquiescent suicide. Many of these suicides go unnoticed. Irene's case raises many concerns and questions about institutionalization and quality of care in such facilities and about the vulnerability of older women in our society.

If we are to significantly reduce the incidence of assisted suicide and acquiescent suicide among older women in America, we must do everything we can to educate and enlighten people about gender issues and suicide. We must change our attitudes about older women in this country. We must come to view older women as worthwhile human beings who have given much to society and who deserve the chance to live a meaningful and dignified life in their later years. It is time that we socialize women in this country to see themselves as important and valuable people who do not always have to sacrifice their own lives and happiness for the men in their lives and for their society.

|"Most suicides are preventable."

SUICIDE CAN BE PREVENTED BY INTENSIVE PSYCHOLOGICAL TREATMENT

Andrew E. Slaby

Most people who commit suicide do not want to die but see no other solution to ending their pain, Andrew E. Slaby maintains in the following viewpoint. Many suicides can be prevented, he contends, if therapists treat the individuals' depression aggressively and early and if the individuals have the support of their family and friends. Slaby is a clinical professor of psychiatry at New York University and New York Medical College.

As you read, consider the following questions:

1. According to Slaby, what percentage of all people who commit suicide suffer from major depression?
2. When is the risk of a suicide attempt greatest, in the author's view?
3. Who is at greatest risk for suicide, according to Slaby?

From Andrew E. Slaby, "Psychiatric Treatment of Suicidal Outpatients," *Lifesavers*, Fall 1995. Copyright ©1995 by the American Foundation for Suicide Prevention. Reprinted with permission.

E valuating and managing suicidal outpatients has long made clinicians fearful. Now, as managed and capitated care continues limiting hospitalizations and outpatient treatments, clinicians have become even more anxious about treating patients who are suicidal. Fortunately, a few basic principles of patient management greatly facilitate treating self-destructive outpatients and preventing their suicides.

It is not always possible to prevent suicide, but in most instances the impulse can be significantly reduced when clinicians, patients and patients' families understand the factors that impact suicide risk. Hopelessness, more than depression, predicts suicide. Patients who suicide do not want to die; they simply want to end their pain. When they can see another way to end the pain, they use it. People kill themselves when they feel there is no alternate way to ameliorate their anguish. Many of these deaths could be avoided if these individuals had received aggressive treatment, psychopharmacological therapy, and had their social supports rallied to assist them.

The majority of suicides had psychiatric diagnoses that, if identified and treated, would have diminished the risk of suicide. When initially seen, all patients should be asked if they have ever considered suicide, if they are currently suicidal, and if they have ever made an attempt. Developing a plan for managing suicidal impulses begins with the therapist's first encounter with the patient, or arises during the course of treatment when patients fail to respond to diagnostic-specific treatments.

Characteristics of Suicidal People

Risk Assessment   Approximately 60 percent of all suicides suffer major depression, and 15 percent of the patients with major depression die by suicide. Twenty percent of the people who suicide suffer disorders with a strong affective component, such as a dysthymic disorder [a form of depression], post-traumatic stress disorder, or schizoaffective disorder. Of the remaining 20 percent who die, a few are so-called "rational" suicides. It is notable that over 10 percent of those stating they want to suicide because they have an incurable illness do not have the illness; instead they have a monosymptomatic delusional disorder with the false belief that they have a fatal illness.

Study after study confirms that most individuals who commit suicide suffer from depression. Such affectively ill patients, as a group, are especially creative as artists, politicians, and entrepreneurs; their loss to suicide represents not only a loss of life but society's disproportional loss of their talents. Individuals who are gay—especially adolescents—or who have anxiety disorders or learning disorders are at increased risk. An unrecognized learning disorder such as attention deficit hyperactivity disorder (ADHD) can lead to poor school performance despite superior intelligence. A child whose best efforts fail first becomes demoralized, and then falls hopeless as teachers and family fail to recognize the disorder. Some young people self-medicate ADHD or depression with recreational stimulants (e.g., speed or cocaine) or alcohol, further enhancing their impulsivity and risk.

ROOM FOR HOPE

When teenagers consider suicide, they are far less likely than adults to be expressing the idea that they wish to *end* their lives. They are more likely to be considering suicide as a means to *solve the problems* of their lives. Although it's sad that the ending of a life would ever seem to be a solution to life's problems, understanding this dynamic leaves room for hope: If a troubled teen comes to see another way to solve his or her problems, suicide can cease to be an option.

Bernard Frankel and Rachel Kranz, *Straight Talk About Teenage Suicide*, 1994.

Hospitalization   Most individuals with suicidal thoughts do not require hospitalization; only when their desire to die or impulsivity is great is this necessary. Their suicide risk is greatest shortly after a recent suicide attempt, especially if they have a plan to try again if no relief is forthcoming. Hopelessness, psychosis, absence of social supports, substance abuse, and impulsivity all indicate an increased need for observation and sometimes restraint in a protected environment. Extremely suicidal patients, even in a hospital, may require "arms length" observation to prevent self-harm.

DRUGS AND OTHER THERAPY

Psychopharmacotherapy   In most instances, appropriate psychopharmacotherapy remarkably reduces suicide risk. If the immediate risk of impulsive suicide is exceptionally great, or if symptoms fail to respond to medication, electroshock therapy may be needed.

Most suicides result from fundamental changes in neurotransmitters in the brain that impair perception and affect, resulting in a sense of hopelessness and impulsivity leading to attempts that end in death. The neurochemical defect appears in most cases to be a deficiency of serotonin reflected in a decrease in its principle metabolite, 5-hydroxyindole acetic acid, in the cerebrospinal fluid. This decrease is associated not only with suicide but also homicide. Regardless of their diagnosis, individuals with decreased brain serotonin are also at risk for homicide and for severe and impulsive suicide attempts.

A new generation of antidepressants—the selective serotonin reuptake inhibitors (SSRIs)—specifically remedy serotonin deficiency, improving impulsivity, depression, eating disorders and obsessive compulsive disorders, and reducing symptoms of other disorders which increase suicide risk. The wide safety margin of these SSRIs reduces the hazards of overdose seen with older antidepressant drugs.

WHO IS AT RISK?

Social Support People at greatest risk for suicide are the most socially isolated: particularly divorced, single, or separated men in late life. As adolescents, gay youth do not have support for their gender identity, resulting in their over-representation among adolescent suicides. Support groups for HIV-positive patients, gay youths, and single parents reduce some stress by reducing isolation and allowing sharing of coping skills.

Psychoeducation Patients, families, clergy, caregivers, and others should be taught to recognize individuals at risk, and they should be educated to the role of medication, therapy, and social support in reducing suicide risk. Weight loss, social isolation, sleep disturbances, impulsivity, decreasing work and school performance, and agitation indicate worsening depression. Lack of plans for the future and giving away of prized possessions suggest an evolving plan to die.

Access to Help All patients at risk should be provided with the therapists' phone numbers, their backups, and places to call if neither respond in a timely manner. Lack of access to help at a time of despair may result in panic, anger and impulsive acts.

Realistic Goals The anxiety of caregivers and family members is reduced by mutual understanding of the limits to what is possible. Most depressions respond to antidepressants—many with the first drug chosen—but side effects can limit choice and dosage. The suicide risk may increase in therapy when patients' energy returns before their feelings of hopelessness, helplessness, and worthlessness abate. Schizophrenia, on the other hand, has the same lifetime risk of suicide as major depression, but a somewhat worse prognosis. What works at one point in the course of treatment may not be effective at another point, and management of the illness needs to be altered as circumstances dictate. In some instances, a long time is required for diminution of the desire to die. Even more time may be required to restore or acquire a lust for life that, in itself, would counter a desire to die.

A PAINFUL EXPERIENCE

Surviving Suicide   Loss of a loved one to suicide is perhaps the most painful of human experiences. The pain of the loss of someone to suicide is never totally ameliorated. It is always there, and the survivor's eye is quick to find it. It only becomes tolerable as the thread of loss is woven into the fabric of the survivor's life with threads of more happy moments. Few understand that the death is seldom self-determined, but rather driven by a distortion of perception by a biochemical defect.

Surviving is wrought by confused feelings. Guilt, grief, anger, and despair increase survivors' own risk of self-inflicted death. Each day they may play the game of if's: "What if I said or did that?" "What if I didn't?" Survivor groups help those left behind to learn what feelings to expect, and to learn the course of grief.

Most suicides are preventable if the psychiatric disorders responsible for clinical symptoms and impulsivity are identified early and treated aggressively, and psychosocial stress factors are reduced through therapy. However, a clinician is not omnipotent. Profoundly despairing people can lie about plans and hoard medicine even if prescribed cautiously. The best care for potentially suicidal patients is initial and recurrent assessment of risk, timely intervention, and the provision of support to those especially at risk, regardless of the presence of symptoms.

| "Some suicide may legitimately be prevented, but not all. Arguments for the view that all suicide should be prevented are unacceptable."

SUICIDE PREVENTION IS NOT ALWAYS APPROPRIATE

Victor Cosculluela

In the following viewpoint, Victor Cosculluela argues that in most cases, coercive suicide prevention measures such as involuntary hospitalization are not warranted. Even if an individual considering suicide is mentally ill or ambivalent about suicide, he contends, these are not necessarily valid reasons for suicide intervention. Suicide may be justifiably prevented only in narrowly prescribed circumstances, he maintains. Cosculluela is the author of *The Ethics of Suicide*, from which this viewpoint is taken.

As you read, consider the following questions:

1. According to Cosculluela, why should people with mental illnesses be permitted to realize their desire to commit suicide?
2. In what ways does the "cry for help" theory fail to justify attempts to prevent suicide, in the author's view?
3. In Cosculluela's opinion, why is the fact that a person's desire for suicide is fleeting an unjustifiable reason for preventing the suicide?

From *The Ethics of Suicide* by Victor Cosculluela (Camden, CT: Garland Publishing, 1995). Reprinted with permission of the author and publisher. Footnotes in the original have been omitted here.

Authors from various disciplines have brought forth reasons for preventing all, or at least virtually all, suicide. We will consider these arguments in an attempt to determine whether or not, and in what circumstances, others should prevent a suicide from realizing his intentions. We shall reach a moderate conclusion: some suicide may legitimately be prevented, but not all. Arguments for the view that all suicide should be prevented are unacceptable. . . .

PREVENTING SUICIDE

I will assume that totally uncoercive suicide prevention measures need no justification. For example, merely presenting the would-be suicide with one's anti-suicide position requires no justification. Suggesting a psychotherapist for the person who seeks relief from his suicidal impulses also requires no justification. For the remainder of this viewpoint I will have in mind coercive preventive measures (e.g., involuntary hospitalization, medication, etc.). . . .

PSYCHOLOGICAL ARGUMENTS

Mental Illness: By far the most important psychological argument with respect to suicide prevention is the claim that suicide prevention is justified since suicide is always or at least virtually always a manifestation of some form of mental illness. We are told by Erwin Ringel that the suicidal option is almost always chosen under "pathological circumstances or under the influence of diseased feelings." Further, George Murphy asserts that so-called "rational" suicide is a rarity since most persons who commit suicide are "suffering from clinically recognizable psychiatric illnesses often carrying an excellent prognosis." From this some are led to infer that the therapist must not only make clear to the patient that, in the words of Alan Stone, he "believes such behavior arises from the patient's illness"; he must "do everything he can to prevent it, enlisting the rest of the staff in this effort." Further, the claim is made that suicidal intent "must not be part of therapeutic confidentiality in a hospital setting."

However, there is a great deal of disagreement on the relation between suicide and mental illness. First, even some of those who accept the claim that perhaps most of those who attempt suicide are, as John Moskop and Tristram Engelhardt write, "limited in their ability to think and act rationally by some mental illness" admit that "it would be extremely difficult" to justify the claim that all suicide attempts are products of mental illness. Further, psychiatrist Thomas Szasz claims that the view that suicide is a manifestation of mental illness is "both erroneous and evil": erroneous since "it treats an act as if it were a happening"; and evil because it "serves to legitimize psychiatric force and fraud by justifying it as medical care and treatment." Finally, some psychiatrists take a moderate view, regarding many suicides as mentally ill, while allowing that many make realistic estimations of their options. It is therefore not surprising that after examining the psychiatric material pertaining to suicide, Margaret Battin reaches the following conclusion: "There is clearly no consensus on the frequency of mental illness in suicide or suicide attempts"; in fact, estimates of the percentage of mentally ill among suicides have ranged from as low as 20% to as high as 100%. However, one point on which there is widespread agreement is that relatively few suicides are psychotic. (It would be ironic if most suicides were psychotic since, on some estimates, the suicide rate for psychiatrists is almost seven times that of the general population.)

NO JUSTIFICATION

Even if we accept the claim that the desire to commit suicide is a manifestation of some form of mental illness, that in itself would not justify preventive measures. The desire to produce a comprehensive metaphysical system might be (and no doubt has been) a manifestation of mental illness, but that in itself would not justify others in preventing its realization. Even the desire to recover from one's mental illness might be a by-product of the illness, but surely no one would suggest that this justifies perpetuating the patient's illness. So even if one could show that all suicidal desires are products of mental illness (which is clearly not the case), that alone would not justify preventive measures.

Although these examples show that the fact that a desire arises from mental illness is not in itself sufficient to justify the coercive prevention of its realization, one might claim that the self-harming aspect of suicide, when combined with the presence of mental illness, justifies the coercive prevention of suicide. However, even this claim is false, for we do not always consider it appropriate to prevent those with mental illnesses from realizing their desires, even when those desires are related to their illnesses and their fulfillment would cause the agent harm. For example, even if we discovered that a person's religious practices (e.g., fasting) were due in part to some minor neurosis, we would not (other-regarding factors aside) consider it appropriate to prevent the person from engaging in these practices, even if such practices were harmful to the agent. . . .

THE CRY FOR HELP

A second psychological thesis that is used to justify coercive sui-cide prevention measures asserts that potential suicides wish to be saved; suicidal behavior is a "cry for help." Suicidologist Ed-win Shneidman is the main proponent of this view: "Individuals who are intent on killing themselves still wish very much to be rescued or to have their deaths prevented." Consequently, suicide prevention consists essentially in recognizing that the potential suicide is ambivalent between his wishes to live and his wishes to die, then "throwing one's efforts on the side of life."

PATERNALISTIC INTERVENTION IN SUICIDE

Paternalism is defined as the abridgement of an individual's lib-erty or other rights in order to promote his or her interests, good, happiness, needs, values, or welfare. We restrain the child from touching a hot stove; we oblige the motorcyclist to wear a helmet when riding on the highway. For their own good, we do not allow people to duel, to prescribe their own medications, or to purchase air for scuba diving unless they meet specific quali-fications. And we do not allow them to commit suicide. . . .

Suicide-prevention activities are usually justified on two pater-nalistic grounds: impairment of judgment and harm. However, in some cases suicide is rationally chosen, and death is not a harm. In such cases, *paternalistic* prevention of the suicide is im-possible, since genuine paternalism serves, rather than thwarts, the individual's interest, and prevention would only serve the in-terests of onlookers or of others in the society as a whole. In these cases paternalism does not call for suicide prevention, but forbids it.

Margaret Pabst Battin, *Ethical Issues in Suicide,* 1995.

This attempt to justify coercive suicide prevention measures is problematic. In support of this view, one might appeal to the fact that a high percentage of would-be suicides appreciate be-ing saved. However, this would only provide a limited defense since some survivors express bitterness over their "rescue." Fur-ther, it is doubtful that those who attempt to commit suicide in ways that make it easy for others to save them fall into the same class as those who attempt suicide in ways which make it nearly impossible for others to save them. The claim that someone who committed suicide by firing a shotgun into his mouth was com-municating a desperate "cry for help" seems quite implausible; it is unlikely that those who want to be rescued would make it virtually impossible for others to rescue them.

However, there is an even more serious problem with the cry for help justification of coercive suicide prevention measures. Shneidman's view is that potential suicides have serious doubts about suicide even though they also have pro-attitudes toward suicide. However, this in itself does not justify suicide prevention. Whenever one makes a difficult choice, it is likely that one will still have doubts, but this in itself does not show that others are justified in preventing us from carrying out our decisions. When somebody makes a career choice, he may have serious doubts about the wisdom of his choice, but such doubts do not allow others to prevent him from carrying out his choice. . . .

THE TRANSITORINESS OF THE SUICIDAL DESIRE

A third psychological thesis, which is repeated quite frequently in the literature, claims that the wish to die by suicide is usually fleeting: "The desire to terminate one's life is usually transient. The 'right' to suicide is a 'right' desired only temporarily," Murphy writes. From this a momentous conclusion is immediately reached: "Every physician should feel the obligation to support the desire for life."

Here again it would be a mistake to use an invalid argument of the following form: since most potential suicides have a certain characteristic, this in itself justifies treating all potential suicides as if they had that characteristic. Even if the desire for suicide is transient in most cases, that in itself will not justify the claim that all suicide should be prevented. One can easily imagine cases in which individuals think long and hard on the suicidal option before embracing it.

Further, why should the simple fact that a desire is transient justify others in preventing its realization? The desire to do something very good for others might be fleeting, but that in itself does not show that others are justified in preventing its realization. Clearly, the lifespan of a desire does not in itself determine whether or not one should prevent its realization, otherwise one would have to say that a transitory desire to do good for others must be frustrated.

The appeal to the claim that most suicide results from mental illness, the appeal to the alleged ambivalence of most suicides, and the appeal to the alleged transitoriness of most suicidal impulses all fail to justify the claim that all suicide should be prevented. Further, since the mere fact that a desire springs from mental illness, the mere fact that one is ambivalent about it, and the mere fact it is fleeting are each insufficient to show that the desire's realization should be prevented, it turns out that appealing to mental illness, ambivalence, or to the fleeting nature of suicidal impulses will not in itself justify suicide prevention in *any case whatsoever*. Further, even if one made an appeal to all three claims (i.e., the mental illness claim, the ambivalence claim, and the transitoriness claim), it seems that that in itself would not justify any preventive measures. Why, then, have so many authors repeatedly appealed to these alleged facts in an attempt to justify coercive suicide prevention measures?

BELIEFS ARE RELEVANT

With respect to the mental illness claim, the reason may be that mental illness is related to something else which is relevant to the question of suicide prevention: the potential suicide's factual (non-moral) beliefs. Whether or not someone has correct factual beliefs is relevant to the issue of paternalistic interference. If, for example, laymen want to take certain drugs in the belief that they will be cured of their ailments, when in fact they would be seriously harmed, laws which attempt to prevent them from obtaining the drugs without prescriptions may be justified. Mental illness enters the picture when we realize the impact it can have on one's factual beliefs; depending on the severity of the illness, one might come to hold ludicrous factual beliefs. For example, one might come to believe the following: "Unless I kill myself, I'll become a werewolf." In cases where mental illness creates factual ignorance which gives rise to suicidal intentions, suicide prevention may be justified. Even in such a case, it would be inaccurate to say that the presence of mental illness justifies preventive measures; the factual errors justify preventive measures; the mental illness simply happens in this case to be responsible for the factual ignorance which is partially responsible for the desire to commit suicide.

Mental illness is also relevant when it prevents someone from acting on his deepest desires, even though it may not involve factual ignorance. One might, for example, be the victim of irrational fears or compulsions which push one toward self-destruction, even though one may also have a rationally formed desire to live. In such cases, preventive measures seem justified. (It should be noted, however, that . . . it is unclear that self-destruction due to compulsions counts as suicide.)

AMBIVALENCE AND TRANSIENCE

As for the appeals to ambivalence (the cry for help model) and the alleged transitoriness of suicidal desires, these claims seem relevant to factual beliefs about one's deepest desires; if one is ambivalent, one may say, "I don't know what I want," and transitory desires often create confusion about what one "really" desires. Paternalistic prevention measures may be justified by the potential suicide's ignorance about his own deepest desires. However, it would be incorrect to say that the ambivalence alone, or the transitoriness alone, justifies preventive measures; rather, factual ignorance which would otherwise be likely to cause self-harm justifies paternalistic preventive measures. Ambivalence and transitoriness are relevant only as possible sources of ignorance.

One might claim that transitoriness is itself directly relevant to the issue of whether preventive measures would be justified in cases of potential suicide. After all, one may *really* want *now* to kill oneself. However, if this desire would only last for, say, a minute, it may seem that that in itself is relevant to the issue of suicide prevention.

It seems to me that if the transitory desire for suicide accompanied (perhaps by causing) the mistaken belief that the desire is enduring, that would indeed be relevant, but only because that would be an instance of factual error. (Presumably, most people would not act on their suicidal impulses if they were aware of the transitoriness of these impulses.) However, one might press the point by proposing a highly unusual case in which a potential suicide *really* wants to kill himself yet is fully aware that this desire is fleeting. If our potential suicide realizes that his suicidal desire is fleeting and if he is in control of himself, then, unless other-regarding factors are at stake, it seems to me that we are not entitled to prevent his suicide. (I am assuming here that would-be preventers know that the potential suicide has the knowledge and self-control in question.) . . . The potential suicide knows that he genuinely wants to kill himself, he knows that his desire is fleeting, and yet he still wants to fulfill the desire. Why should the mere fact that the desire is transient matter in this case when it does not matter in other cases (e.g., cases in which one has transient desires to do tremendous good for society)?

It might be said that in cases of suicidal desire, the transient desire would be terminal if fulfilled. But if death is precisely what the person wants, and if he knows that this desire is fleeting, I fail to see how the *mere* fact of transitoriness counts. Transitoriness is related to factual ignorance (e.g., it may mask one's deeper desires and it might create the illusion that the transitory desire for suicide is actually an enduring desire), but it is only because of this relation that it is relevant to the suicide prevention issue. . . .

OTHER-REGARDING CONSIDERATIONS

So far we have focused only on the would-be suicide. One might, however, try to defend suicide prevention measures on the ground that suicide involves deep suffering for others (e.g., the suicide's family and friends). Naturally, one will have to balance this suffering against the negative features of preventive measures; we are not entitled to prevent people from acting in certain ways on the ground that others would be slightly annoyed otherwise. Further, this justification of suicide prevention will not apply to those would-be suicides who do not have important relations to others.

None of the arguments considered justifies preventive measures in all cases of potential suicide. The psychological arguments from mental illness, transitoriness, and ambivalence turned out to be only indirectly relevant; such features alone never justify preventive measures, but they are relevant to the would-be suicide's factual beliefs and self-control. In that sense, mental illness, ambivalence, and the presence of transitory suicidal impulses are indirectly relevant to the issue of suicide prevention. . . . Finally, the argument which tries to justify suicide prevention measures by appealing to other-regarding considerations will justify some instances of prevention, but not all.

PERIODICAL BIBLIOGRAPHY

The following articles have been selected to supplement the diverse views presented in this chapter. Addresses are provided for periodicals not indexed in the *Readers' Guide to Periodical Literature*, the *Alternative Press Index*, the *Social Sciences Index*, or the *Index to Legal Periodicals and Books*.

Stephen Chapman	"For the Dying, a Better Option than Suicide," *Conservative Chronicle*, May 8, 1996. Available from Box 29, Hampton, IA 50441.
Diane M. Gianelli	"Treat Pain, Avert Suicide," *American Medical News*, September 23–30, 1996. Available from the American Medical Association, 515 N. State St., Chicago, IL 60610.
A.J.F.M. Kerkhof	"Suicide and Attempted Suicide," *World Health*, March/April 1994.
David Lester and J. Bean	"Attitudes Toward Preventing Versus Assisting Suicide," *Journal of Social Psychology*, vol. 132, no. 1, 1992. Available from 4000 Albemarle St. NW, Washington, DC 20016.
Colman McCarthy	"Pain Management vs. Doctor-Assisted Suicide," *Liberal Opinion Week*, October 24, 1994. Available from PO Box 468, Vinton, IA 52349.
Kate Darby Rauch	"My Mom Killed Herself by Mixing Sleeping Pills with Alcohol," *Washington Post Health*, May 17, 1994. Available from Reprints, 1150 15th St. NW, Washington, DC 20071.
Edwin S. Schneidman	"Suicide as Psychache," *Journal of Nervous and Mental Disease*, vol. 181, no. 3, 1993. Available from 428 E. Preston St., Baltimore, MD 21202.
Lonny Shavelson	"What the Dying Really Need," *New York Times*, March 8, 1996.
Suicide & Life-Threatening Behavior	"Suicide Prevention: Toward the Year 2000," Spring 1995. Available from The Guilford Press, 72 Spring St., New York, NY 10012.
Jacob Sullum	"No Relief in Sight," *Reason*, January 1997.
USA Today	"Getting Help for Depressed Teenagers," December 1993.

FOR FURTHER DISCUSSION

CHAPTER 1

1. According to Ernest van den Haag, each person has ownership of his or her life and is therefore entitled to decide when to end it. However, Robert P. George and William C. Porth Jr. contend that human beings cannot be owned, even by themselves; therefore, they conclude, there is no right to suicide. With which viewpoint do you most strongly agree? Why?

2. Based on your reading of the viewpoints by Roger Miner and Robert R. Beezer, do you think the U.S. Constitution guarantees a right to assisted suicide? Why or why not?

CHAPTER 2

1. Christopher Scanlan cites studies by the Centers for Disease Control and Prevention and other researchers that found that the risk of teen suicide increases when guns are kept in the home. David B. Kopel quotes a study by Gary Kleck that found no evidence that gun-control laws had an effect on teen suicide rates and that countries that sharply restrict gun ownership often have higher suicide rates than the United States. After reading the viewpoints, do you think gun availability affects the teen suicide rate? Explain your answer.

2. According to Gary Remafedi, gay and lesbian teenagers face an increased risk of suicide due to their distress over their sexual orientation. Trudy Hutchens contends that other factors are behind the suicides of homosexual teenagers. Both cite studies to support their arguments. Based on information from the viewpoints, what do you think are the strengths and weaknesses of each study? Which viewpoint do you think provides a more accurate view of teen suicide? Why?

CHAPTER 3

1. Robert T. Hall argues that there is no difference between a doctor letting a patient die and helping the patient die; the two deaths are merely described using different words, he maintains. Leon R. Kass contends that there is a significant ethical distinction between the two events. Based on your reading of the viewpoints, do you think there is a difference between cessation of treatment and physician-assisted suicide? Explain your answer.

2. Timothy E. Quill asserts that it is moral and ethical for a physician to help a patient die to avoid a painful death. According to John Paul II, however, it is "false mercy" to help

someone who is suffering end their life, as only God has the right to decide when to end a life. Which argument do you find more convincing? Why?

3. Based on your reading of this chapter, do you think physician-assisted suicide is murder, as Walter Reich contends, or a justifiable end-of-life treatment, as Thomas A. Preston argues? Support your answer with examples from the viewpoints.

CHAPTER 4

1. Ralph L.V. Rickgarn asserts that people who intervene in the lives of troubled or suicidal individuals may be able to prevent suicide. Ann Smolin and John Guinan maintain, however, that often nothing will prevent a person who is determined to commit suicide from ending his or her life. Give examples from the viewpoints in this book of circumstances in which intervention may save a life and circumstances in which it may not. Explain your answers.

2. The American Foundation for Suicide Prevention (AFSP) argues that most terminally ill people who request physician-assisted suicide do not want to die but merely want to avoid the pain and suffering their disease may cause. The AFSP asserts that providing effective pain management gives the patient time to come to terms with death. Timothy E. Quill contends that sometimes pain management is not enough and that suicide may be the only way to achieve true relief from pain and suffering. Which argument do you find most convincing? Why?

3. This chapter lists several possible methods of preventing suicide. Consider each alternative and then list arguments for and against the validity of each one. Note whether the arguments are based on facts, values, emotions, or other considerations. If you do not believe an alternative is a valid method of suicide prevention, explain your reasoning.

ORGANIZATIONS TO CONTACT

The editors have compiled the following list of organizations concerned with the issues debated in this book. The descriptions are derived from materials provided by the organizations. All have publications or information available for interested readers. The list was compiled on the date of publication of the present volume; names, addresses, phone and fax numbers, and e-mail and Internet addresses may change. Be aware that many organizations take several weeks or longer to respond to inquiries, so allow as much time as possible.

American Association of Suicidology
4201 Connecticut Ave. NW, Suite 310, Washington, DC 20008
(202) 237-2250 • fax: (202) 237-2282
The association is one of the largest suicide prevention organizations in the United States. It promotes the view that suicidal thoughts are almost always a symptom of depression and that suicide is almost never a rational decision. In addition to preventing suicide, the group also works to increase public awareness about suicide and to help those grieving the death of a loved one to suicide. The association publishes the quarterly newsletters *American Association of Suicidology—Newslink* and *Surviving Suicide*, and the quarterly journal *Suicide and Life Threatening Behavior*.

American Foundation for Suicide Prevention (AFSP)
120 Wall St., 22nd Fl., New York, NY 10005
(212) 410-1111 • (800) ASF-4042 • fax: (212) 269-7259
Internet: http://www.asfnet.org
Formerly known as the American Suicide Foundation, the AFSP supports scientific research on depression and suicide, educates the public and professionals on the recognition and treatment of depressed and suicidal individuals, and provides support programs for those coping with the loss of a loved one to suicide. It opposes the legalization of physician-assisted suicide. AFSP publishes a policy statement on physician-assisted suicide, the newsletter *Crisis*, and the quarterly *Lifesavers*.

American Life League (ALL)
PO Box 1350, Stafford, VA 22555
(703) 659-4171 • fax: (703) 659-2586
ALL is a pro-life organization that provides books, pamphlets, and other educational materials to organizations opposed to abortion, euthanasia, and physician-assisted suicide. Its publications include pamphlets, booklets, and reports, the handbooks *Life, Life Support, and Death* and *A Pro-Life Primer on Euthanasia*, the bimonthly magazine *Celebrating Life*, and the newsletter *ALL About Issues*.

Americans United for Life (AUL)
343 S. Dearborn St., Suite 1804, Chicago, IL 60604-3816
(312) 786-9494 • fax: (312) 786-2131

AUL is committed to promoting public awareness of the sacredness of all human life, including the lives of the elderly and of comatose patients. It lobbies against the legalization of euthanasia. AUL publishes several books and essays on euthanasia, the periodical *AUL Insights*, and the seasonal newsletter *AUL Forum*.

Canadian Association for Suicide Prevention (CASP)

#201 1615 Tenth Ave. SW, Calgary, AB T3C OJ7
CANADA
(403) 245-3900 • fax: (403) 245-0299
e-mail: siec@nucleus.com
Internet: http://www.web.idirect.com/casp/pmplocx.html

CASP organizes annual conferences and educational programs on suicide prevention. It publishes the newsletter *CASP News* three times a year and the booklet *Suicide Prevention in Canadian Schools*.

Center for the Rights of the Terminally Ill (CRTI)

PO Box 54246, Hurst, TX 76054
(817) 656-5143

CRTI is an educational, patient advocacy, and political action organization that opposes assisted suicide and euthanasia. Through education and legislative action, it works to ensure that the sick and dying receive professional, competent, and ethical health care. Its publications include pamphlets such as *Living Wills: Unnecessary, Counterproductive, Dangerous* and *Can Cancer Pain Be Relieved?*

Choice in Dying (CID)

200 Varick St., New York, NY 10014
(212) 366-5540 • fax: (212) 366-5337
e-mail: cid@choices.org
Internet: http://www.echonyc.com

CID is dedicated to fostering communication about end-of-life decisions among the terminally ill, their loved ones, and health care professionals by providing public and professional education about the legal, ethical, and psychological consequences of assisted suicide and euthanasia. It publishes the quarterly newsletter *Choices* and the Question & Answer Series, which includes the titles *You and Your Choices, Advance Directives, Advance Directives and End-of-Life Decisions,* and *Dying at Home*.

Compassion in Dying

PO Box 75295, Seattle, WA 98125-0295
(206) 624-2775 • fax: (206) 624-2673
e-mail: cid@compassionindying.org
Internet: http://www.compassionindying.org

Compassion in Dying provides information, counseling, and emotional support to terminally ill patients and their families, including information and counseling about intensive pain management, comfort or hospice care, and death-hastening methods. It promotes the view that terminally ill patients who seek to hasten their deaths should not have to die alone because their loved ones fear prosecution if they are found present. Compassion in Dying does not promote suicide, but condones hastening death as a last resort when all other possibilities have been exhausted and when suffering is intolerable. It publishes the newsletter *Compassion in Dying*.

Foundation of Thanatology
630 W. 168th St., New York, NY 10032
(212) 928-2066 • fax: (718) 549-7219 • fax: (914) 793-0813
This organization of health, theology, psychology, and social science professionals is devoted to scientific and humanist inquiries into health, loss, grief, and bereavement. The foundation coordinates professional, educational, and research programs concerned with mortality and grief. It publishes the periodicals *Advances in Thanatology* and *Archives of the Foundation of Thanatology.*

Hemlock Society
PO Box 101810, Denver, CO 80250-1810
(303) 639-1202 • (800) 247-7421 • fax: (303) 639-1224
e-mail: hemlock@privatei.com
Internet: http://www.hemlock.org/hemlock
The society promotes the view that the terminally ill have the right to commit suicide. It supports the practice of voluntary suicide and physician-assisted suicide for the terminally ill. The society does not encourage suicide for anyone who is not terminally ill, and it supports suicide prevention programs. It publishes books on suicide, death, and dying, including *Final Exit,* a guide for those who are suffering with terminal illnesses and who are considering suicide. The society also publishes the quarterly newsletter *Hemlock Time Lines.*

Human Life International (HLI)
7845 Airpark Rd., Suite E, Gaithersburg, MD 20879
(301) 670-7884
The pro-life Human Life International is a research, educational, and service organization. It opposes euthanasia, infant euthanasia, and assisted suicide. The group publishes books such as *Death Without Dignity,* pamphlets, the monthly *HLI Reports,* and the bimonthly *PRI Review.*

National Hospice Organization (NHO)
1901 N. Moore St., Suite 901, Arlington, VA 22209
(703) 243-5900 • (800) 658-8898 • fax: (703) 525-5762
NHO seeks to treat and comfort terminally ill patients and their families at home or in a home like setting, paying special attention to pain management and symptom control. Its philosophy accepts death as a natural part of life. The organization opposes euthanasia and assisted suicide. Its services (available twenty-four hours a day, every day) include support and bereavement care for family members and friends. It publishes the *Hospice Fact Sheet* and the quarterlies *Hospice Journal* and *Hospice Magazine.*

Samaritans
500 Commonwealth Ave., Boston, MA 02215
(617) 247-0220

Samaritans is the largest suicide prevention organization in the world. Established in England in 1953, the organization now has branches in at least forty-four nations throughout the world. The group's volunteers provide counseling and other assistance to suicidal and despondent individuals. In addition, Samaritans publishes the booklets *Elderly Suicide*, *Teen Suicide Information and Guidelines for Parents*, and *The Suicidal Student: A Guide for Educators*.

SA\VE—Suicide Awareness\Voices of Education
PO Box 24507, Minneapolis, MN 55424-0507
(612) 946-7998
e-mail: save@winternet.com
Internet: http://www.save.org

SA\VE works to prevent suicide and to help those grieving after the suicide of a loved one. Its members believe that brain diseases, such as depression, should be detected and treated promptly because they can result in suicide. In addition to pamphlets and the book *Suicide: Survivors—A Guide for Those Left Behind*, the organization publishes the quarterly newsletter *Afterwords*.

Suicide Information and Education Centre
#201 1615 Tenth Ave. SW, Calgary, AB T3C OJ7
CANADA
(403) 245-3900
fax: (403) 245-0299
e-mail: siec@nucleus.com
Internet: http://www.siec.ca

The Suicide Information and Education Centre acquires and distributes information on suicide prevention. It maintains a computerized database, a free mailing list, and a document delivery service. It publishes the quarterly *Current Awareness Bulletin* and the monthly *SIEC Clipping Service*.

Survivors of Suicide Support Program
#301 349A George St. North
Peterborough, ON K9H 3P9
CANADA
(705) 748-6711 • fax: (705) 748-2577

Survivors of Suicide Support Program is a patient advocacy group for the mentally ill in Peterborough and the surrounding area. It works to increase public awareness and understanding of mental illness through education. It maintains a lending library and distributes pamphlets on suicide bereavement.

BIBLIOGRAPHY OF BOOKS

Leroy Aarons — Prayers for Bobby: A Mother's Coming to Terms with the Suicide of Her Gay Son. San Francisco: HarperSanFrancisco, 1995.

Robert L. Barry — Breaking the Thread of Life: On Rational Suicide. New Brunswick, NJ: Transaction Publishers, 1994.

Margaret Pabst Battin — Ethical Issues in Suicide. Englewood Cliffs, NJ: Prentice Hall, 1995.

Margaret Pabst Battin — The Least Worst Death: Essays in Bioethics on the End of Life. New York: Oxford University Press, 1994.

Michael Betzold — Appointment with Doctor Death. Troy, MI: Momentum Books, 1993.

Silvia Canetto — Women and Suicidal Behavior. New York: Springer, 1994.

Victor Cosculluela — The Ethics of Suicide. New York: Garland, 1995.

Donald W. Cox — Hemlock's Cup: The Struggle for Death with Dignity. Buffalo, NY: Prometheus Books, 1993.

Ronald M. Dworkin — Life's Dominion: An Argument About Abortion, Euthanasia, and Individual Freedom. New York: Knopf, 1993.

Bernard Frankel and Rachel Kranz — Straight Talk About Teenage Suicide. New York: Facts On File, 1994.

Herbert Hendin — Seduced by Death: Doctors, Patients, and the Dutch Cure. New York: Norton, 1996.

Herbert Hendin — Suicide in America. New York: Norton, 1995.

James M. Hoefler and Brian E. Kamoie — Deathright: Culture, Medicine, Politics, and the Right to Die. Boulder, CO: Westview Press, 1994.

Paul C. Holinger et al. — Suicide and Homicide Among Adolescents. New York: Guilford Press, 1994.

Derek Humphry — Final Exit: The Practicalities of Self-Deliverance and Assisted Suicide for the Dying. Eugene, OR: Hemlock Society, 1991.

Stephen Jamison — Final Acts of Love: Families, Friends, and Assisted Dying. New York: Putnam, 1995.

Susan Kuklin — After a Suicide: Young People Speak Up. New York: Putnam, 1994.

Gerald A. Larue — Playing God: Fifty Religions' Views on Your Right to Die. Wakefield, RI: Mayer Bell, 1996.

Antoon Leenaars — Treatment of Suicidal People. New York: Hemisphere, 1994.

David Lester	*The Cruelest Death: The Enigma of Adolescent Suicide.* Philadelphia: Charles Press, 1993.
Barbara Logue	*Last Rights: Death Control and the Elderly in America.* New York: Lexington Books, 1993.
Eric Marcus	*Why Suicide? Answers to 200 of the Most Frequently Asked Questions About Suicide, Attempted Suicide, and Assisted Suicide.* San Francisco: HarperSanFrancisco, 1996.
Rita Marker	*Deadly Compassion: The Death of Ann Humphry and the Truth About Euthanasia.* New York: William Morrow, 1993.
John L. McIntosh	*Elder Suicide: Research, Theory, and Treatment.* Washington, DC: American Psychological Association, 1994.
Jonathan D. Moreno, ed.	*Arguing Euthanasia: The Controversy over Mercy Killing, Assisted Suicide, and the "Right to Die."* New York: Simon & Schuster, 1995.
G. Steven Neeley	*The Constitutional Right to Suicide: A Legal and Philosophical Examination.* New York: Peter Lang, 1994.
New York State Task Force on Life and the Law	*When Death Is Sought: Assisted Suicide and Euthanasia in the Medical Context.* New York: New York State Task Force on Life and the Law, 1994.
Timothy E. Quill	*Death and Dignity: Making Choices and Taking Charge.* New York: Norton, 1993.
Gary Remafedi, ed.	*Death by Denial: Studies of Suicide in Gay and Lesbian Teenagers.* Boston: Alyson Publications, 1994.
Ralph L.V. Rickgarn	*Perspectives on College Student Suicide.* Amityville, NY: Baywood, 1994.
Sue Rodriguez and Lisa Hobbs Birnie	*Uncommon Will: The Death and Life of Sue Rodriguez.* Toronto: Macmillan, 1994.
Edwin S. Schneidman	*Definition of Suicide.* Northvale, NJ: Jason Aronson, 1995.
Lonny Shavelson	*A Chosen Death: The Dying Confront Assisted Suicide.* New York: Simon & Schuster, 1995.
Ann Smolin and John Guinan	*Healing After the Suicide of a Loved One.* New York: Simon & Schuster, 1993.
Joni Eareckson Tada	*When Is It Right to Die? Suicide, Euthanasia, Suffering, Mercy.* Grand Rapids, MI: Zondervan, 1992.
Kate Williams	*A Parent's Guide for Suicidal and Depressed Teens.* Center City, MN: Hazelden, 1995.
James K. Zimmerman and Gregory M. Asnis, eds.	*Treatment Approaches with Suicidal Adolescents.* New York: John Wiley, 1995.

INDEX

prevention
  begins with education, 131, 154-55, 170
    of physicians, 140, 142-43
  and need for research, 64-65, 157
  as not always appropriate, 172-79
  and psychological treatment, 167-70
  and support groups, 83, 170
  and social attitudes, 158
    toward elderly, 159-60, 163, 164-65
      especially women, 160-61, 162, 165-66
  see also intervention
  rates of, 58, 61
  as rational choice, 19-20, 174, 175, 176
  and risk assessment, 168
  teen, 137
    and alcohol, 78, 79
    by car exhaust poisoning, 58
    and family problems, 68, 74, 133
    and guns
      exaggeration of use in, 56-59
      in home, contribute to, 51-55, 78, 79
    and homosexuality, 60-65, 82, 169
      exaggeration about, 66-69
      need for research into, 62, 64-65
    and hopelessness, 79-81, 83
    rates of, 71, 74
      comparative, 53, 57-58
    schools may help prevent, 153-57
      with peer recognition of danger, 127
      with response to crisis trauma, 155-57
    see also depression; drugs
Suicide and Life-Threatening Behavior (McIntosh), 163
Suicide in Later Life, Recognizing the Warning Signs (Osgood), 159
Sullum, Jacob, 20
Szasz, Thomas, 173-74

terminally ill, the, 22, 33, 34, 37, 101
  disempowerment of, 102
  lack right to assisted suicide, 43, 44
  unnecessary suffering of, 102, 106, 152
  see also comfort care; individual rights; suicide, physician-assisted; withdrawal of life support

United States, 53, 57, 63, 157
  Constitution
    does not recognize right to die, 41, 43, 45, 96
    Equal Protection Clause, 40, 45, 46
    and right to suicide, 33-40
      according to Fourteenth Amendment, 35, 36
      as not fundamental, 42-43
      for patients not on life support, 33, 37-38, 45, 46
      and rational relationship test, 44-45
      see also individual rights; Washington statute
  Court of Appeals, 33, 39, 98, 99
  Department of Health and Human Services, 61, 67, 82
  gay men in, 64
  passive euthanasia in, 104
  and right to refuse treatment, 90
  Supreme Court, 39, 42, 43, 44
    Schweiker v. Wilson, 46
United States Catholic Conference, 45

Vacco, Dennis C., 34
van den Haag, Ernest, 16, 27, 31, 32
  supports right to suicide, 25, 26
  weak arguments of, 28, 29-30
Vatican, the. *See* Declaration on Euthanasia; Second Vatican Council

Ward, Andrea Young, 86
Washington Post, 58, 59, 134
Washington statute, 44, 45, 47, 119
  see also *Compassion in Dying . . .*
Wickett, Ann, 160
withdrawal of life support, 33, 37, 38, 90, 120
  and comatose patients, 32
  as constitutional right, 45
  does not guarantee "natural" death, 38
    or pain-free dying, 106, 146, 147, 148, 149
  elderly can be pressured into, 39
  is fundamentally different from active euthanasia, 46, 98, 104
    con, 91, 121, 148
  as legal hastening of death, 33, 37, 150
  as not equivalent to suicide, 109
  should be available to all, 40
World and I magazine, 38